Behavioral Issues in Horses: Why Do They Do That?

~NICOLE BRICKNER~

ISBN-13: 978-1532887925
ISBN-10: 1532887922

Edited by Corrina Peterson

Cover design by Christa Holland/*Paper and Sage*
Cover image by Juraj Kovak/shutterstock.com

For Rush and Madison, who taught me that patience and understanding are the keys to life. Without these qualities, we are lost.

CONTENTS

ACKNOWLEDGMENTS

This book exists because of the two most influential animals in my life: my Morgan gelding Rush and my Labrador retriever mix Madison. I was blessed to have them in my life to teach me about patience, compassion, dedication, and respect. Both of these beautiful animals had personality quirks that could, at times, make them frustrating to work with. They needed a unique approach to their training and to their everyday lives to get the rewarding results that only come with time. They taught me that no two animals are alike, and that sometimes you need to think outside of the box and work with the individual in terms they can understand and appreciate. Without the influence of these two angels in my life I would not even be close to the success I experience working with animals.

Next I need to thank my family. My wonderful parents for all of their support along the bumpy road of life. For wiping away the tears of frustration and giving the hugs of encouragement. For pushing me when I wanted to give up and catching me when I fell, for celebrating in my accomplishments and helping me become who I am. I would not be the woman I am today without your unwavering love and support. Also my fiancé Brad who has been supportive and understanding of the lifestyle of a horse trainer. I know I am not easy to live with and I thank you for standing by me all these years.

I also need to thank my past lesson instructors and professors who taught me and shared their knowledge of horses with me. Those who pushed me and never let me give up. Those who recognized my talents and helped me progress as a rider and a trainer. I could never thank you enough for teaching me to not only train the horse but respect the horse as the amazing and beautiful creature it is. For teaching me that we usually learn more from the horse than they will ever learn from us. For proving to me that we never know it all and there is always more to learn from every horse and every owner.

Lastly, I need to thank Corrina Peterson for helping me complete this huge accomplishment. Your editing and assistance in making this the best book possible was invaluable. You gave me the push I needed to believe in myself and take this leap.

INTRODUCTION

"I was drawn to horses as if they were magnets. It was in my blood. I must have inherited...a genetic proclivity toward the equine species. Perhaps a quirk in the DNA...makes horse people different from everyone else, instantly divides humanity into those who love horses and the others who simply don't know." ~Allen J. Hamilton

I have had the privilege of owning two exceptional animals with personalities and tendencies that would have severely limited their time in this world had they landed in the wrong hands. They were difficult to work with and understand, but were also unbelievably gifted and remarkable animals. They required a level of patience and understanding that exceeded anything I had ever come across or ever have since. They also gave a level of love and loyalty that I learned to cherish and hold dear.

The first was my beloved Morgan gelding, Rush. He entered my life as a just gelded, green-broke, four-year-old with an attitude a mile long. I was a confidant, horse-crazy teenager. Rush challenged me, taught me, put me in my place, made me cry, made me laugh. He broke my leg, my ribs, and my fingers (all of which I look back and know were due to my shortcomings and inexperience). He taught me perseverance, dedication, humility, courage, and above all to never stop trying or believing in my dreams. Over the course of our nineteen years together, he went from an aggressive, head-strong, difficult horse, to a quiet, loving, and safe beginner lesson horse. This transformation would not have happened had I given up on him, as so many said I should. So many life lessons I would never have learned without the encouragement from a select few who saw the same potential in him that I did. He taught not only me but, later in his life, dozens of other horse-crazy kids to respect and appreciate horses. I lost Rush in November of 2013 after nineteen amazing years by his side. I have never felt such a loss or felt so blessed to have been part of such an amazing horse's life.

The second was my beautiful lab mix, Madison. I got her as a puppy my senior year in college and she was a huge change from the outgoing, boisterous Golden Retriever I had grown up with. Madison was such an introverted and timid girl. She was quirky and shy. She hated loud noises and sudden movements, and was scared of just about everything. I had to coax her out of her shell. She eventually became more outgoing with people she knew but was forever timid with strangers and hid behind me any chance she could. Some people would have found her to be frustrating and complicated. I saw her for the loving, loyal, beautiful, intelligent, caring, and amazing girl she was. I lost my Madison in November of 2013, after twelve years of friendship and guidance.

These two greatest influences in my life departed within five days of each other. Letting go of my beloved teachers, saying goodbye to two of the best things that ever happened to me, inspired me to write this book.

If I can help any of the other talented, loving, gifted animals that need only to be understood and given time and patience to evolve into the amazing creatures they can be, then this book will have been a success.

If I can help people to understand that there are always reasons for so-called difficult or bad behavior, that we can figure it out and get past it, and that we can find all the good the animal has to offer, I will have succeeded.

My purpose for writing this book is simply to help horse owners learn to better understand and communicate with their horses, to remove the communication barrier and build a relationship of mutual respect and understanding, to teach people how to read and interpret what the horse is trying so desperately to tell them. In doing this, we eliminate so many of the most common problems that arise between horse and human.

Throughout this book, my philosophy of "it is never the horse's fault, it is always ours" is emphasized to its fullest. If you are not willing to recognize and accept that fact, you need not read any further. Let me explain.

When we choose to become a horse owner/rider/trainer/parent, we assume the responsibility of a higher standard of care. This involves and requires greater awareness, understanding of normal horse behavior, and vigilance in identifying and recognizing potential hazards and dangerous circumstances that could result in what we characterize as "negative outcomes."

We are imposing ourselves into the horse's life. They did not ask us to handle them, ride them, show them, race them, or do any of the other hundreds of things we do to control their lives. If an accident occurs or a mistake is made, it is the human's fault for putting the horse in the situation. We handled circumstances poorly, did not prepare our horse or ourselves properly for the task at hand, or ignored what our horse was trying to tell us. In this respect, you need to take full responsibility for anything negative that happens to you, your horse, or other people and objects. Take responsibility and learn from it, grow from it, embrace it as a stepping stone to becoming a better horseperson.

Know that everyone makes mistakes and accidents happen, but it's how we handle these occurrences and move forward that matters. There is not a horseperson or trainer alive who hasn't made dozens of mistakes, taken dozens of falls, gone to bed sore and frustrated. It is how we learn from and handle these rough times that allows us to become more successful and capable. Remember, if we want to take credit for the good, we need to accept responsibility for the bad.

I must get at least a dozen phone calls a week – some from strangers, some from past or current clients – asking me how to "fix" a problem they are having with their horse. This is one of the biggest problems we must address: *They are asking the wrong question.* Instead of asking how to fix something, we need to ask why it is occurring in the first place. Only then can we successfully solve issues with our horses. We cannot ask for a solution to a problem without first identifying the actual problem. You wouldn't go to the doctor and simply say, "my leg hurts, fix it," would you? The doctor needs to know the details, such as where does it hurt, when did it start hurting, was there something that made it start hurting, etc. In other words, the diagnosis comes first, then the treatment. Herein lies the potential for a disconnect between horses and humans. We want a solution, but we first need to determine the cause. Instead of asking, "How can I get my horse to do/or not do something," we first need to know why they are or are not doing it. This is not as simple as it may seem, because for every behavior problem or bump in the training road there are numerous possible causes. The goal is to get to the root of the problem and come up with a solution for that specific situation – diagnose, then treat.

This isn't always easy, and we may not always be correct in our assessment right away. I have spent many nights staring at my ceiling racking my brain trying to figure out why something is not going right with the training of one of my horses. I evaluate the situation over and over, and suddenly an idea will come to me. Then I can't wait to test my theory the next day and see if I correctly solved the issue and can move forward in the training process. This is the exciting part, getting inside the horses head and figuring things out! Trust me, once you get a feel for it you will be hooked. It's so much easier and less stressful modifying behavior if you know the cause of it.

In the following chapters I will go over general horse behavior, addressing the most common behavioral problems and their most common causes. I'll also cover other important information relating to horses' thought- and decision-making processes, and how to positively and productively influence them. I will examine the possible physical, mental, and emotional reasons for various horse behaviors, as well as how to properly deal with them and move forward. Of course we can't cover everything in one short book, but my goal is to get you thinking like a horse and problem solving by "walking a mile in their hooves," so to speak. If you can learn to see things the way they might be seeing them, then the chances of coming up with a positive solution to the problem are much better.

Reading this book will not make you a horse trainer any more than reading a book about airplanes will make you a pilot. My goal is to help you to better understand your horse and deal with some possible issues productively and safely. In some cases, you may need to contact a professional trainer to help you solve a problem, especially with some of the more dangerous behaviors. Even then it will help you to understand what is going on and what is needed to help the situation.

Note: All names, and some minor details that do not affect outcomes, have been changed to respect the privacy of the people and horses in the case studies.

CHAPTER 1
BEGINNING WITH A SOLID FOUNDATION

"Your horse will forgive you for your mistakes, your inconsistencies, your flaws and faults, but it will not forget. If you cause fear or pain, you will see the memory of those actions reflected in their eyes forever as a constant reminder to never commit that sin again. Those who see this reflection, those who feel the pain in their chest from knowing they have failed their equine partner, and those who choose to learn from it and to try harder and be better, will continue to grow and become truly connected with their horses. Those who cannot or will not see their faults reflected back at them will never truly grow or learn. Who will you be?"
~Nicole Brickner

We get so much from our relationship with the horse, the least we can do is try to understand them on the deepest levels, to search inside ourselves to find that unspoken connection and truly communicate with our horse. You cannot see things from your horse's perspective if you are unwilling to recognize and acknowledge the incredible animals they are and the instincts that drive them. When you can take a step back and see the world through their eyes you will begin to understand what they need from us to be successful in the training process.

To work with a horse successfully, we first need to understand horses and their natural instincts that can interfere with us accomplishing what we would like to do. Only then can we use these instincts to our advantage. We need to understand why a horse might be reacting the way it is and how to modify these reactions. Working with horses on a level they can understand is key. This chapter will also go over important factors that can negatively affect your relationship with your horse, and ways to eliminate or minimize these factors. Finally, we'll cover the best ways to work with your horse to get the most out of your sessions.

Understanding horse instincts

Routine

Horses are creatures of habit; they do best with routine and consistency. They thrive on a schedule and an understanding of their place in your world. If we provide a horse with a stable and secure environment and a clear explanation of their job, things will usually go well. Everything from feeding on a regular schedule, plenty of accessible clean water, a chance to stretch their legs and have fun, a sense of security in their life, all of these contribute to your horse's comfort level with their environment and with you. Carry this consistency into their chosen discipline and your horse will thrive. If they know what is expected of them, if they can be confident in your responses to the good and the bad – reward and discipline given fairly and justly – they will enjoy you and their work.

Prey vs. predator

Horses are prey/flight animals. They will choose to leave any stressful situation if given the opportunity. This concept is hard for us to understand since we, as humans, are predators. We also tend to surround ourselves with other predators, dogs and cats being the most prevalent. Looking at a situation the way a horse may be seeing it, as a prey animal, can be difficult for us. We are not accustomed to thinking this way or dealing with this reaction from horses. We need to recognize and understand that they will try to run away from stressful situations, and that this can heavily impact our interactions with them. We cannot become angry or frustrated with the flight response, we need to learn to deal with it and act and react appropriately. We need to learn to modify our horse's flight response through muscle memory training, trust building exercises, and developing a strong bond. We also need to remember that we can never completely eliminate this innate part of their being.

Hierarchy

Horses are instinctively herd/hierarchy animals. They are programmed to live in groups and establish a "pecking order" within that group. There are definite rules and regulations established within a herd of horses. First and foremost, you have an "alpha" horse. This is the boss of the herd. They have full control and command of all other horses within their area. They are in control of the food, the water, the shelter, and the entire turnout area. They have the authority to move the other horses around the pen on a whim. The rest of the herd will fall into the pecking order in a manner similar to ranks in the military. You will have a second in command, third, and so forth. All the way down to the most submissive horse in the herd.

This mentality carries over into their relationship with people. If we want to control the horse and the situation, we need to assert ourselves as the alpha. A horse's underlying personality type and ranking within the herd will determine how difficult this will be. If you have a dominant horse, you will have a little harder time establishing leadership. If you have a submissive horse, you will have a little easier time with this. The key to establishing leadership is establishing a mutually respectful relationship with your horse. You get what you give. You cannot expect to receive respect from your horse if you do not give it respect in return. Quite simply, horses are bigger, stronger, and faster than we are, so we need to acknowledge and accept that in order to successfully establish a respect-based relationship.

Controlling a horse's movement, where they go and how fast, is a basic aspect of establishing the leadership standing. This is one of the reasons that round pen work and ground work are so important. Moving your horse's feet in accordance with what you desire establishes dominance. This is not always easy, horses will challenge and refuse and you need to know how to deal with this.

Respect is not the same as fear

Let me emphasize that respect is completely different from fear. Your horse should never fear you. This will breed a whole slew of behavioral problems on its own. The goal is to never cross this line with the horse. I implement very safe and natural methods within my training. Escalation in methods to discourage behavior should increase in accordance with the horse's reaction to discipline for a behavior. Every horse is different. Some, usually the more submissive horses, only need a sharp word and a bump in the halter, while some can tune you out and ignore most efforts at discipline and behavior modification. With these horses, which normally have an alpha personality, you will increase the deterrents for the behavior in increments to find the point at which they no longer wish, or find it beneficial, to continue the undesired behavior. If the horse in any way, shape, or form sees the behavior as successful or productive, they will continue the behavior.

For instance, if your horse gets to do what they want for even a few moments before you adjust the behavior, they will view it as a success. If your horse breaks into the trot when they have been asked to walk, and they are able to trot for even a few strides before being brought down to the walk again, they will be encouraged to continue that behavior.

On the other hand, if your chosen consequence for the undesired behavior is not at a level that the horse sees as a sufficient deterrent, they will also continue the behavior that they prefer, in this case picking up a trot whenever they wish.

Individual personality

Identifying your horse's personality is another key to progress with training or to address a behavioral problem. First, understanding whether your horse is an alpha or dominant horse or a more submissive animal is highly important. There are all sorts of in-between levels of dominance and submissiveness, and you must identify where your horse falls in this spectrum. Next is identifying other key personality traits. Is your horse curious, shy, nervous, bold, friendly, aloof, pushy, timid, confident, hesitant, etc? Identifying how your horse behaves – with other horses, with you, with new situations, with surroundings, with unexpected or unfamiliar objects or noises – will all help you relate to and work with your horse. Use this knowledge to adjust your riding and training methods to best suit your horse's personality.

Considering *our* behavior

No one method for addressing a problem will work on every horse. We need to allow for modifications that take the horse's personality into consideration. This can cause major frustrations if you are trying to use a method that you learned through a video or book. You may do it correctly, and still it may not be effective with your horse. Another problem with following a book or video to train, improve, or modify behavior in your horse is the lack of ability of the average horse owner to pick up on important body language of the horse.

A trainer or experienced horse person is able to see and respond to changes in a horse's body language. The horse tells us through body language what is going on in its mind. If we do not pick up on the subtle messages they are offering, we can totally blow an exercise with a horse, and even cause or worsen a bad situation.

Black and white

One of the first major building blocks for better communication with your horse is the understanding that horses work best with a black and white set of boundaries. No gray areas, just black and white. Or, if you prefer, remember it as the "always or never" rule – no sometimes, no maybe. If you are going to allow it, you must be willing to always allow it. If you are not going to allow it, you must be clear and consistent that it is never allowed. By occasionally allowing a behavior you do not necessarily approve of or are too tired or busy to correct, you set the scene for confusion and frustration for your horse.

If there will be times when a certain behavior is not allowed, you must be firm and consistent in never allowing it. You cannot occasionally let your horse exhibit rude, pushy, and disrespectful behaviors if you are going to discipline those same behaviors at a later date. Even behaviors that are not acceptable in certain situations but are normally not a problem need to be handled consistently. For example, if you allow your horse to itch his face on your body after you dismount or finish the session at home, you cannot expect him to not to do it when you are wearing your expensive show clothes. This may also be a problem when he tries to scratch his face on your little cousin and knocks him to the ground. Again, the horse will be blamed and most likely disciplined for its actions. You can see how this simple behavior, when handled differently under different circumstances, can cause problems and confusion. There are hundreds of behaviors you might allow in certain circumstances but not in others. If there is ever going to be a time when you will not allow or will not accept a particular behavior, you need to never allow it! Yes, this involves some awareness and forethought on our part, in addition to consistency. If we do not abide by this rule, we will cause confusion and frustration within the horse. Confusion and frustration breed behavioral problems.

If you will expect a certain behavior and/or performance from your horse, you must consistently require it, no matter how tired, crabby, or sore you may be. You cannot allow a lackluster performance one day because you're tired and then demand a stellar performance the next day because you feel ambitious. Tailor your training session to what you are willing to do that day. Don't compromise your horse's sanity by bouncing back and forth between expectations on a day-to-day basis. Imagine if your boss changed expectations of you on a day to day basis, but didn't tell you what day they expect what performance. That would be frustrating, correct? This is the reason for the "black and white" or "always/never" rule.

Consistency

Next, consistency is key. Always ask the same way for the desired response. Give it time, don't necessarily expect an immediate result or correct answer to your request. Still, be consistent and persistent in your cues and handling of the horse. Do not change the way you are asking in an attempt to elicit a correct response. If you want your horse to respond to a certain cue, you must stick with it until that response is given, and then take the cue away. So many times I see people giving all sorts of random cues trying to get the desired response. Stick to a cue, make the right thing easy and the wrong thing difficult, and wait for the desired result. After that, be consistent every time you ask for that response. Ultimately, this will create a trusting and confident relationship between you and your horse. If your horse knows who you are and what will be asked, and that it will be clear, consistent, and fair, things will go much smoother.

What does it mean to "make the right thing easy and the wrong thing difficult"? It simply means opening the correct door and closing the incorrect door. For instance, if you are asking your horse to back, you want to close the go forward, go left, and go right doors with your hands, seat, and legs. This creates a "road block" for your horse if it tries to go forward, left, or right. Keep the door behind the horse open, inviting, and resistance free, so they want to choose that door. Encouraging the horse to go through an open door instead of trying to break through a closed one is much easier for you and your horse.

What I often observe is that people tend to give the horse several "open door" options and simply discipline the horse for choosing incorrectly when they have no clue which door they should go through. If you ask your horse to back but only close the go forward door, your horse will try all possible doors – left, right, and back – and get discouraged when you discipline or fail to reward an attempt to go through an open door. It's the same as if you asked your host at a party where the bathroom was and they said, "the open door down the hall on the left," and as you walk down the hall almost all the doors are open. Now imagine if you entered the wrong door and got in trouble for it! Frustrating, right?

Self-control

Another important requirement for working with horses is relaxation – yours, to be specific. Breathe and be calm whenever you are working with your horse. There is no room for temper or emotion. You must remain focused, quiet, and level-headed. If negative emotion gets involved, things will always go downhill from there. Your horse does not understand the reason for your anger or frustration, just that it is there and it is very disturbing to them. If you find yourself losing your calm, take a time out and resume when you have settled again.

A suitable partner

Compatibility and suitability are important aspects to consider when deciding if your horse is right for you and/or your discipline of choice. An ill-suited pairing leads to frustration for both horse and owner, and ultimately culminates in behavioral issues.

Compatibility refers to the match between you and your horse.

If you are not a good match with the horse, either physically or personality-wise, you will almost certainly run into problems along the way.

Physical compatibility

Let's look at physical compatibility first. When searching for a horse or deciding if we have the right horse, we need to take into account physical size.

The rider's weight is one of the most important factors. If you weigh 300 pounds, you need a more substantial horse to carry you. Height of the horse is not as important as bone and muscle structure in this case. You can be fine with a shorter horse if it has a more solid, substantial bone structure and a stockier physique. It does not matter if you get a 16-hand horse if it is a narrower, finer boned animal with small feet, it will not be able to carry you for lengthy amounts of time without strain on its body and joints. Ultimately this will lead to a physically and mentally unhappy horse. You need a horse that is built to carry more weight. Additionally, if you weigh 100 pounds soaking wet, you might want to consider a smaller horse. A taller, stockier horse will generally be more difficult for you to handle, tack up, etc.

Height is the next important factor. If you are six feet tall, you will probably want a taller horse to balance out the equation. If you do not weigh much and are a taller rider, you can still ride a smaller or more fine-boned horse, it's just that the overall balance and picture are sometimes viewed as awkward. On the other hand, if you are five feet tall you may want a shorter horse for a more balanced picture and ease of grooming, tacking up, mounting, etc. Whatever your combination of physical characteristics, whether it is tall and thin, tall and stocky, short and thin, short and stocky, be honest and take those physical attributes into account.

One difficult situation is finding a suitable mount for growing children. Some people go the route of finding a mount that will most certainly be outgrown, and they do so knowing they will need to sell this horse and upgrade in size along the way. Others choose to buy a mount that the child will "grow into." This can also work, but you may have a more difficult time during the years where the horse will be a little too big for the child to handle and take care of on their own.

The next area to address is any possible physical limitations of the rider. If you have a bad back, bad hips, arthritis, asthma, etc., or possibly are just getting older and not able to physically do as much as you used to, keep these things in mind when purchasing or making the decision to keep or sell a horse. For instance, if you have bad hips an especially wide horse might not be the best choice. If you have asthma a very high energy horse may not be the best choice, and so on.

Age and experience

Another element to consider in the horse/human pairing is the age and experience level of both horse and rider. In general, young, green horses do not pair well with beginner riders. The combination of an inexperienced horse with an inexperienced rider can lead to confusion and frustration for everyone involved. (A green horse generally refers to a horse that is relatively inexperienced under saddle or within a certain discipline.) It works best to have an experienced horse for a beginner rider to learn with, or an experienced rider to work with and teach an inexperienced horse. It plays into the old saying of not letting "the blind lead the blind" – that hardly ever goes well!

Additionally, an extremely quiet, older horse might not pair well with an advanced and energetic teenage rider. The rider will want to ride aggressively and extensively, while the horse may be too laid back and physically incapable of keeping up with the rider's energy and riding level, causing both physical and emotional frustrations.

On the other hand, a quieter more relaxed rider will not pair as well with an energetic and highly athletic horse. They will constantly be butting heads as the rider will want to have a quiet and relaxing ride and the horse will get extremely bored and frustrated.

The examples could go on for pages, but the general idea is to honestly assess and appropriately match your age, skill level, and ability to handle different horse behavior when pairing a person with a horse. Are you a little nervous and want a "been there, done that" horse? Or are you a confidant, adventuresome rider who will get bored easily with a finished and predictable mount? These are things to think about carefully before choosing a horse.

These are just guidelines, and there are certainly exceptions to every situation. I know tall people who ride shorter breeds and short or lightweight people who handle bigger and stronger breeds with ease. There are some weaker or more physically compromised riders who handle energetic and strong horses easily. Some timid riders may also grow and learn from a horse that challenges them. A quieter more experienced horse may teach an adventurous and wild person to settle down and focus. You must be honest with yourself about your physical attributes, what you truly desire from a horse, and possible problem areas. Then buy wisely, not impulsively.

Personality

Now you need to identify what type of personality you want from a horse. Are you energetic, loud, and intense? You may want an equally energetic, strong-willed, confident horse. Are you quiet, reserved, passive? You will probably want a quieter, more laid back, easygoing horse. Again these are guidelines, certain odd combos of personality do sometimes work, but those are exceptions to the rule. Identify yourself honestly and pick a horse accordingly.

Most recreational horse owners, especially women and children, have the underlying desire to have a close, loving relationship with the horse. We want them to love and adore us as much as we do them. If you implement the structure and work with your horse in a manner similar to what is described in this book, there will be a higher chance your horse will truly enjoy your company and want to be with you.

Love is a controversial topic in this context, but I do believe horses are capable of loving people. I have seen horses desire to be with certain people, accomplish feats and exhibit behaviors out of such a strong bond with a person, that it can only be explained by love. Will your horse love you? That is out of your hands. You can establish trust and respect. Through those, and with time, if the compatibility is correct your horse may exhibit signs of love or affection towards you.

Compare it, if you will, to dating. You can enter a room and immediately be drawn to someone. Their physical appearance, their personality, everything about them makes you want to be with them. Does that mean they will feel the same? As most of us have found out, it does not. No matter how badly you want that person, or in this case, your horse to love you, no matter how hard you try to be perfect, they may not. This does not mean you cannot have a good working relationship and be a great team, but as with our human-to-human relationships, you cannot force your horse to "love" you. It's not personal, it's just the way things are and you need to accept it.

One of the best things you can do is understand your horse's personality and accept it for what it is. There are certain horses out there that would truly like to keep their human interaction minimal and work on a professional level, and have a strong dislike for anything further. Respect that, and if you are not satisfied with owning a horse with that type of personality, then find the horse that craves attention and enjoys time with people. Conversely, if you want to keep your riding and relationship with the horse strictly professional and unemotional, seek out a horse that exhibits those same tendencies.

Horses exist on both ends of that spectrum, and many in between; you just have to spend the time looking. I have worked with and owned all varieties. I have a mare right now that will leave her hay and her friends in the paddock and happily come to the gate for anyone! She is an absolute sweetheart, she adores people. I have also had horses that literally radiate their distaste for anything that has to do with people or interaction with people. They are compliant and do their job but nothing further. They exude a "get it over with and leave me alone" attitude. This is no different than people who would just rather read a book or stay home and watch a movie, rather than interact with others or be social. There's nothing wrong with it, it's just a personality type.

It's important to understand that, if you are truly unhappy with or incompatible with the horse you have, it is ok to move on and find your horse a more suitable owner and yourself a more suitable horse. Trying to force something with a horse will end poorly with both of you being miserable.

Intended activities

Suitability in your intended activities refers to your horse's ability to accomplish the type of riding you would like to do. Physical suitability to the task is important. In general, certain breeds and breed characteristics lend themselves well to certain disciplines. Quite simply, you may want to pick a breed that excels in the discipline you have chosen. There is a reason most reining and western pleasure champions are well-bred quarter horses; that phenomenal huntseat, dressage, jumping, and eventing horses are usually Appendix or Warmblood crosses; that most saddle seat horses are Saddlebreds and gaited Morgans; that endurance trail horses are Arabs or Arab crosses. The physical attributes of these breeds lend themselves to the work in which they excel.

Again, there are exceptions. There are Morgans who win reining classes, Arabs that win western pleasure, Quarter horses that are wonderful huntseat horses, etc.

Once you've narrowed it down to a certain breed, be sure to consider any physical limitations an individual horse may exhibit. A horse with some conformational front leg flaws may do just fine in pleasure and flat work, but could come up lame in the rigors of jumping. A senior horse may have or may develop arthritis issues that are not a problem for your trail riding ambitions, but could limit their quality of movement in the show pen.

Finally, your horse should like their chosen discipline. Even if they are bred for it and have the body for it, that does not mean they will enjoy it. Just as not all tall people love basketball, not all tall horses love to jump. Just because both your parents are great at hockey and you have the correct body type to play it well, doesn't mean you will want to. Your beautifully bred cutting and roping horse may hate being around cows. It happens. The important point is to look and buy or keep and sell wisely. Don't try to fit a square peg in a round hole, you will likely end up with problems.

Establishing a working relationship

Before we get into the common behavioral problems that can occur, we need to understand how to properly work with the horse in the first place. As I mentioned earlier, consistency is vital. With consistency comes dependability and relaxation. To establish a good working relationship with your horse, you need to have a game plan. The worst thing you can do is just jump on and ride with no rhyme or reason to the outing. If we do not have a purpose to our work we tend to take our horse's suggestions on what we should do for the day. When this happens, our horse develops a viewpoint that they are ultimately in control of their works. Unfortunately it doesn't take long for this mindset to occur, and for the horse to become, in our eyes, difficult to work with.

Let me give you several examples. You are casually warming up your horse along the rail without giving clear direction. (Working on the rail refers to riding along the wall or fence line in an arena setting.) On this particular day the horse feels like cutting the corners of the arena. While you are not actively pushing him into the corner and asking for inside bend and softness, your horse takes the opportunity and leans into the corner, cutting the arena smaller. By letting him do this, as you were not actively steering in the first place, you are telling him he is in charge of direction. Next, your horse starts to walk faster. You can tell he has energy and wants to trot so you comply and ask for the trot. Your horse feels like moving out so you continue the warm up at the posting trot while continuing to allow your horse to cut the corners in the arena. After several laps your horse shortens his stride and starts to slow down, as he has expended his excess energy, so you start to work on the jog.

You have now started to focus on the ride and decide you want to work on bending through the corners. You ask and your horse refuses. When you apply more inside leg and ask more firmly he pins his ears and walks faster, even picking up the trot. Irritated, you pull him back to the walk and ask out loud, "what is wrong with this horse today!" Can you see the problem? You let your horse call the shots for the first twenty minutes of your ride until you decided to be in charge, so now he is arguing with you and he has every right to! This is an example of an everyday oversight or occurrence that has seemingly mild consequences. If this routine of allowing your horse to suggest what should be done continues, you will end up with some full-fledged behavioral problems.

Here is the solution: Be mindful and control every aspect of your time with your horse, from the moment you slip on that halter to the moment you put him away.

Another element of controlling the situation is simple. If you can tell your horse wants to do one thing, do the opposite. If your horse is drifting to the rail, work away from the rail. If he is drifting in and cutting the corners, push him to the rail and into the corners. If he wants to walk, trot, or canter fast, ask him to slow the pace. If he wants to be lazy and sluggish, move him out and extend his gaits. If you do these simple things on a regular basis, you establish a leadership role that your horse will rarely question. This is a reaction that comes very naturally to trainers and experienced riders – do the opposite of what your horse is suggesting they would like to do.

Have a plan for your work. What do you want to accomplish? What are you going to work on? Have a goal for the day, all of these things will shine through and show your horse that you have a purpose for the work. They will pick up on your confident and purposeful guidance and willingly work with you. When your horse feels as though the work has no purpose they get bored, crabby, frustrated, irritated, etc. It would be the same as you going to work or school with no goal or purpose for being there. Would you want to be there? Would you feel it was a waste of time and energy and would you be crabby for the day? Wouldn't you rather be out playing or at home relaxing instead of participating in a pointless activity? Apply this concept to your horse. You need to give him a job and purpose if you want him to be excited and cooperative about his work. Be consistent with this simple step and the results will amaze you.

Implement these rules and guidelines, work with a horse suited to you and your discipline, plan your everyday handling and training of your horse. These are all ways to avoid and/or minimize any potential problems that could arise, and will ultimately help you establish a good working relationship with your horse built on mutual trust, respect, and confidence in each other.

CHAPTER 2
THE ROOT OF THE PROBLEM

"A barn is a sanctuary in an unsettled world, a sheltered place where life's truer priorities are clear. When you step back, it's not just about horses – it's about love, life, and learning. We honor our horses for their brave hearts, courage, and willingness to give. Indeed, horses have the hearts of warriors and often carry us into and out of fields of personal battles. Those who know them understand how fully a horse can hold a human heart."~Lauren Davis Baker

When looking at a negative behavior, we need to not think of it as the horse being naughty, rather that the horse is making a decision we do not agree with. It's not personal, it's simply your horse disagreeing with you. Since they cannot have an oral argument with us on the best way to proceed, they tell us in other ways that they prefer their decision over ours. This is no different from us not agreeing right away with rules or requirements in different areas of our lives, and needing them explained and enforced to change our thoughts on the situation.

Keeping in mind how generous the horse is in even allowing us to guide them and control their movements, how do we convince them to further accept our handling and curb the disagreements that inevitably occur when we have a difference of opinion? What do we do when a problem arises regardless of how well we think we are working with our chosen equine partner? What to do when we purchase a horse and weeks later stumble across a significant behavioral issue?

The first thing we need to do is understand the root cause of the issue. The following assessment will help you to do that.

Physical pain

There are many reasons a horse may resort to a negative behavior, the most common and first to always consider is possible physical pain/discomfort. This can include sore back, withers, hips, stifles, hocks; poorly fitting tack that may be pinching or causing uncomfortable pressure points; mouth or bridle/bit problems; or any variation or combination of these issues.

You can do the initial evaluation yourself, and you must start at the beginning. Does your horse show signs of displeasure when being groomed, including picking the feet? The horse may pin ears and/or step away when certain areas of the body are touched. Pay close attention to the withers, back, and hip area. Does the horse refuse to or reluctantly allow you to pick some of his hooves but not others? He may have joint pain that is preventing him from willingly giving you that leg/hoof.

Does the horse pin its ears and/or step away when being saddled or cinched up? (Cinching up or tightening the girth refers to the tightening of the strap that holds the saddle in place.) Your saddle, pad, or girth may be causing some discomfort. Does your horse normally take the bit well, but now is refusing? He may be experiencing oral discomfort.

You can see here how important it is to know your horse and their normal mannerisms. Some horses have developed poor habits/manners while being groomed or saddled. If your horse typically behaves in a negative manner during grooming and tacking up, it may be much more difficult to use those cues as an indicator of pain. You'll need to identify this in your horse before using this method to determine if there is a physical problem. Be careful to not confuse general bad manners with a negative reaction that may be associated with physical/pain or discomfort during grooming, saddling, cinching up, or bridling.

If you determine that the cause may be physical, you should consult a veterinarian to diagnose and treat the problem. You can also consult with your veterinarian about appropriateness of chiropractic treatments and saddle fitting possibilities for your horse. Determining if your horse is in need of a veterinarian, chiropractor, or a saddle fitter should be your focus.

If you're satisfied that your horse has no identifiable physical pain/discomfort issues during grooming or tacking up, it is time to further evaluate the problem. We will next shift our focus to identifying more specifics about the behavior. Do they object right after you mount and ask for forward motion? Do they only 'misbehave' when you ask for collection, or ask for the canter, or when circling left? Do they act up whenever you pick up on the reins?

Try to pinpoint the trigger or pattern associated with the behavior; this will help to narrow down the possible causes. After you've narrowed down the behavior pattern you must brainstorm for possible reasons. Again, take your horse's normal demeanor and personality into account when evaluating the situation. Have they always been crabby when mounted and first walking off, or when asked to canter, etc.... or is this a new development?

If the situation in question has always been a point of irritation for your horse, they have probably just escalated that into a more proactive symptom. For instance, if your horse has always pinned their ears and swished their tail when asked to canter, the progressions to now bucking, rearing, bolting, etc., when asked to canter might just simply be your horse saying more firmly, "I don't want to." You still need to discover the root of the problem and the source of your horse's sourness, but it is not a "new" development.

If your horse has always willingly cantered off when asked and has now all of a sudden started to object when asked to canter, we would consider that a new development which would suggest a major change in something that is occurring at that time. Categorizing these things will help to diagnose the cause of the problem and come up with a suitable solution. After you have identified the problem as an escalation of prior sourness or a new development you need to evaluate the situation further.

With a sudden or new development where there was previously none, our thoughts turn to a physical cause first. Something about the maneuver is possibly causing pain/discomfort for the horse. Have you started using new equipment? This could be a source of discomfort for the horse.

At this point, it may be time to consult a veterinarian. Give them your educated observation points first and then have your horse evaluated for any possible physical causes for the behavior. If you find a physical cause then proceed with a treatment and hopefully the behavior will go away. Unfortunately, sometimes even after you have removed the physical cause the behavior can persist. At this point, you will need to treat it as a learned negative behavior

Behavior as root cause: Conditioning and habits

If you have ruled out a physical cause, or continue to have the problem after a physical cause has been identified and successfully treated, or when dealing with an escalation behavior, it may be necessary to consult a trainer experienced in evaluating and handling horses with behavioral issues that have no physical cause or continue once the physical cause is no longer present. They can help you figure out the cause, which can range from boredom, to playful mischief, to a dislike for their work environment, or anticipation of remembered pain. Then, they can help you formulate a plan of action for curbing the behavior. In an escalation case, they might also find a root physical problem or simply identify the horse's distaste for the activity in the first place.

Keep in mind that most behavioral issues don't start overnight. Usually the horse has been giving numerous signs and you were not understanding or seeing them until the behavior escalated to a point that is now completely unacceptable or downright dangerous.

For example, perhaps you have been working on speeding up your horses back-up. You are pushing your horse faster and harder than they are willing to go at this point. Your horse is not soft enough or mentally ready to increase the speed of the back. The horse will usually start throwing his head and refusing, with every ride you insist and now the horse starts to hop a little when the head throwing occurs. You back off slightly, for just a moment, and then insist again, the horse hops higher, again you hesitate, the behavior makes you a little nervous, then insist again. This time the horse executes a half rear, you get a little more nervous and get off. The next day you try again, the horse refuses and you hesitate every time before insisting on the maneuver until your horse has started to rear higher and higher. You get off again, incredibly nervous now, as you should be. You wait a few days then get on again, as soon as you start to pick up on the reins they start to head toss and hop and quickly escalate into an impressive rear. You dismount and call a trainer, claiming your horse all of a sudden started rearing and you need it fixed now.

With a behavioral cause, the horse rarely goes from nothing to all out in a day. It is usually a progressive process that can take several rides, or even years, to develop to a point where you no longer know how to or feel comfortable handling the situation. In many of these cases, you can also be inadvertently teaching and rewarding the unwanted behavior.

Emotional response

Finally, a horse may exhibit a negative behavior when experiencing an emotional response. Fear, frustration, genuine panic – all of these can elicit an emotional behavioral response.

When a horse responds out of emotion, the behavior is usually sudden and irrational. They may combine many different behaviors such as pulling back, bolting, running into people, objects, other horses, fences, etc. Emotional responses usually have a very specific body language – elevated head and neck, wide eyes that roll around in the socket, body tremors, increase in respiration and heart rate, and an inability to be handled or ridden in a normal manner. Emotionally triggered behavioral responses can be the most dangerous to deal with, as the horse can genuinely (and irrationally) act and react with little to no regard for their own wellbeing, let alone yours.

Negative experiences and bad environments can cause these emotional responses. Past abuse can manifest into anxiety and fear issues that may be triggered by various circumstances. Additionally a specific accident during activities such as trailering, crossing water, jumping, etc… can create future emotional responses during those activities. Being pushed too hard too fast can cause emotional responses including irritation, frustration, and even anger. This will also cause the horse to want to leave the situation. (Remember, running away is the natural behavior for the prey animal.) Lack of proper food, water, and shelter can also manifest into emotion based responses stemming from fatigue, hunger, and thirst. Emotion based responses are by far the most erratic and potentially dangerous behaviors the horse can exhibit.

CHAPTER 3
BUCKING

"We have almost forgotten how strange a thing it is that so huge and powerful and intelligent an animal as the horse should allow another and far more feeble animal to ride upon its back."   *~Peter Gray*

Bucking, in simple terms, refers to when a horse lowers its head, rounds up underneath itself and kicks out with its hind legs. There are many variations and levels of severity to bucking. A "crow hop" is when the horse lowers the head and "humps up" and then hops on all fours, similar to a bird hopping across the ground. Horses may also simply "kick out" with one hind leg or the other. Needless to say none of these variations are pleasant to deal with, whether it's during groundwork or under saddle.

Bucking is a horse's natural reaction to trying to rid itself of a predator. A horse bucks in an effort to "get the mountain lion off its back." This natural instinct can be carried over into our present day interactions. When a horse feels the need to "rid itself" of a problem, the buck can be a common "go to" maneuver. If your horse finds anything about its work unpleasant, uncomfortable, or threatening, it may buck in response.

Horses may also incorporate a "feel good" buck on occasion. This is usually accompanied by a head toss and a burst of energy. This buck is not meant to rid the horse of anything, simply to express happiness or exuberance. Nevertheless, we need to teach the horse that this behavior is not acceptable when being handled or ridden.

As stated earlier, a physical problem, including but not limited to a sore back, withers, hips, or a poorly fitted saddle, may all cause this behavior to occur. Again, this would be the horse's attempt to get the predator off its back. Something is causing pain or discomfort and the horse feels the need to rid itself of this problem.

The following case studies illustrate some of my personal experiences in dealing with the issue of bucking and the methods used to curb the behavior.

Belle's story

Belle came to me as a three-year-old that needed to be started under saddle. She was a fairly quiet horse with a few rude and pushy tendencies, but nothing alarming. Starting out went well, she moved through the ground work and ground driving with flying colors, and we moved on to saddling. Now, I have a strict rule about bucking under saddle. I allow it briefly the first time the saddle is put on and the horse is sent forward, either on the lunge line or in a round pen, simply to allow them to understand that the saddle is not going to come off with any evasive maneuvers. After that, and about ninety percent of the time, the horse never does buck at all, it is NOT allowed. Well, that first time with the saddle on, I sent Belle forward and she did buck quite a bit, impressive actually, but then we were done with it. It never happened again... until almost a year later.

I had Belle back in part-time training to get her going in the show pen in western pleasure and horsemanship. She was doing quite well. One day I saddled her up and swung into the saddle. Not two seconds later she was bucking, and HARD. I brought her head around, disengaged her hips and stepped her back end around quickly. As we walked off, her back started to relax and we had a good session. The next ride, it happened again. I checked saddle fit, no problem there. I disciplined her for the behavior a little more harshly, incorporating a slap with the reins across her hindquarters and a more aggressive leg, with no positive results. The behavior continued for a few more rides. (Disengaging the hips refers to yielding the horse's hindquarters off of your leg pressure and asking them to quietly perform crossover steps with their hind legs.)

As stated earlier, the first thing to look for when a negative behavior starts is a physical reason. Is something causing discomfort and/or pain, and is that the cause of the issue? I called my vet, and after a full evaluation we decided to set up a chiropractic adjustment. It turned out Belle's back and hips were, in laymen's terms, quite out of whack. After the adjustment I got my sweet Belle back and training progressed. A few months later the bucking started again, so I scheduled another adjustment and it worked like a charm. We determined that Belle was extremely sensitive through her back and, even though the saddle fit well and the workload was reasonable, with the collection and conditioning work needed to become a competitive show horse she needed adjustments every eight weeks to keep her comfortable.

Of the possible causes, these mild physical problems often have the simplest solutions, but complications can arise. If the behavior, in this case bucking, is aggressive enough, or if the rider is not experienced in riding out bucks strong enough to get the rider off, a physical problem may turn into a learned behavior which may very well continue after the physical problem is resolved. At that point, even though the physical pain associated with saddling, mounting, riding, etc., is gone, the horse remembers that they were able to get their rider off and may do so whenever any physical, mental, or emotional distress occurs, however mild, in

31

the future. Do not confuse this with the first few rounds back to work, as the horse may buck initially until they recognize that the physical unpleasantness is no longer there. If it has become a learned behavior it will continue after the horse has had time to realize the pain/discomfort is gone.

Additionally, the horse may have learned to fear the back pain and start to object to handling or saddling at all, which may lead to the need to "restart" the horse when the physical issue is resolved. This process is usually less involved than was the initial training and is just needed to reset the horses mind.

Austin's story

I received a phone call from a distraught man one day saying that his warm blood cross had decided that "he no longer liked to be ridden!" Austin had taken to bucking off every single one of the last half dozen riders who had gotten on him, the last of whom was a clinician. The man was desperate and couldn't find anyone else willing to ride the horse. He had a thorough physical exam and saddle fit done and there were no issues found. Before this, Austin had been quite a nice gelding that had very few problems with being ridden. I agreed to come see him.

I conducted my own physical exam, made sure all tack fit correctly, watched him move on the lunge line. Satisfied that there were no issues in those areas, I proceeded to get on. Now, mind you, I had quite an audience, as word had gotten around that a new trainer was going to try riding this "bucking bronco." All the barn boarders and their friends came to "watch the show." I am happy to report that there was no show. Austin never once bucked as I rode. The secret? Keeping his mind occupied! He was bored with a capital B! Every time he started to get bored, I could feel him physically prepare to buck and I would distract him with a new cue, transition, etc. I had Austin in training for several months and the horse never bucked. There were many times I could feel him think about it, but when distracted with other productive exercises he would quickly change his mind.

Unfortunately, Austin did prove to be a horse that would routinely test any new rider. If you did not keep him occupied, you were going for a rough ride at best, hitting the dirt at the losing end of it. Given this attribute his owner decided to sell him to a trainer who very successfully rides and shows him herself in dressage and jumping.

Horses are very intelligent animals that enjoy mental stimulation. If they are not given enough to think about, their minds will wander and they'll come up with other entertaining ways to amuse themselves. These are rarely amusing and entertaining behaviors to their riders/handlers. Keep your horse's mind busy and a lot of their negative antics will simply disappear.

Mabel's story

Mabel was a cute little paint pony, just a hair under 14 hands tall, that had been living the life of leisure in her owner's field. That is, until her owner's husband decided one day that he was going to saddle her up and ride her. He didn't have much experience and Mabel hadn't been ridden in years but, of course, he thought he could easily handle the situation. Mabel did beautifully, she stood nicely to be saddled and mounted and off they went in the field. Now, as most people know, horses, especially pudgy ponies, have this wonderful trick of "holding their breath" when being saddled, and letting it out later so the girth is nice and loose, which is way more comfortable for the horse. Unfortunately, the unsuspecting husband did not know this. As they picked up a trot through the field the saddle started to slide….

Her rider came off and Mabel tore through the field, terrified and bucking, with the saddle hanging under her belly. Finally, too tired to continue, the pony was caught and unsaddled.

The next day, the wife, knowing all too well what a bad experience like that can do to an animal, saddled up Mabel cautiously and got on. Relieved at the pony's relaxation, they walked around the field quietly. No longer worried, she cued

Mable up to the trot and, after only a few strides, Mabel took off bucking, eyes wide with fear. Rider came off and Mabel again continued running and bucking until she was too tired to continue. This time the saddle did not so much as slip but Mabel's anxiety got the best of her. After numerous attempts, they called me. Every time she was asked to go faster than a walk Mabel fell apart. I agreed to help. They brought Mabel the next day.

Oh lord was this pony cute and sweet and wonderful! I fell in love with her within days. We started slowly in the round pen and worked our way up to trotting with the saddle on, but without a rider yet. Sure as could be, I saw the fear enter that mare's eyes and she took off bucking around the round pen. I let her. I talked to her quietly and waited for her to stop. I then went up to her, rubbed her all over and we walked until she had caught her breathe and relaxed. Again I sent her forward at a trot, and again she panicked and took off bucking, but not nearly as long this time. Using this method over the course of days, we kept decreasing the amount of running and bucking Mabel did until one day it didn't happen at all. She was now ready for a rider again. I went through the same process as we had done without a rider and received a considerably more reasonable response, until eventually I got no negative reaction at all. I did not try to prevent the behavior, I just sat on her and let her realize it was all ok, and she did, in her own time, realize that nothing bad was going to happen.

The emotional bucker, whether out of fear, anger, frustration, or any other combination of these emotions is by far the hardest to help. Simply because we, as humans, have little patience, and that is what these troubled horses need. Their emotions are real and if we try to deny them and/or prevent them we will never solve the problem. Only by addressing the emotion with patience, understanding, and dedication will these horses ever get past the roadblock in their own mind. Keep in mind that this emotional roadblock could take weeks, months, or even longer to resolve.

These are only a few stories about actual bucking problems, the different circumstances that caused these particular horses to resort to bucking, and how I addressed and ultimately resolved those problems. There are literally dozens of variations and combinations of problems that can result in bucking, so be patient and find the cause so you can start to modify the behavior. If you feel you are in over your head, please enlist the help of a professional and work with them to help your horse get past this unwelcome and often dangerous behavior.

CHAPTER 4
REARING

You and your horse. His strength and beauty. Your knowledge and patience and determination and understanding and love. That's what fuses the two of you onto this marvelous partnership that makes you wonder, "What can heaven offer any better then what I have here on earth?" ~Monica Dickens

A rear can be defined as any time horse's front hooves leave the ground together and the weight is over the hindquarters. As with all behaviors, there are many different levels of rearing, from the tiny bunny hop of an excited barrel horse ready to run the pattern, to the full height rear of a highly upset equine. The rear is arguably one of the most dangerous negative behaviors a horse can exhibit, simply because the likelihood of injury to the rider increases with the height of the rear.

Most in the horse community have seen the horrific result of a rearing horse, either losing its balance or rearing with enough force to flip over and/or fall, usually on top of its rider. This almost always results in severe injury to the rider, and oftentimes the horse as well. This image, whether seen in person or heard about secondhand, burns a picture in your brain. Now let's take a step back and consider the more common scenario: most horses that have a tendency to rear will never end up falling or flipping over. But, why take the chance? This behavior, whether occasional or frequent, small hops or full rears, needs to be addressed.

Again, the physical causes of rearing are numerous, and can include problems within the mouth, poorly fitting tack, especially the bridle, and overbitting the horse (using a bit that is too severe for them either physically or mentally). Certain maneuvers, such as backing or over-collection, may cause pain in a horse with sore back, hips, hocks, etc. The first step, as always, is to go through the evaluation to determine whether there is a physical source causing the issue. If you feel the source may be physical, consult your veterinarian and takes steps to address that issue.

Rearing is often triggered by riders who are too aggressive with their hands, are asking something that the horse cannot do or doesn't understand, and over-collection to the point of physical discomfort. In this case, it is the rider's awareness and skills that need attention.

A horse may also rear due to pent up energy and excitement. You have probably seen the excited speed horse straining against a tie down before the start of its run. We have all seen the racehorse that rears in the starting gates in anticipation of the race. A horse that is extremely energetic or excited but is held back or made to wait by their human counterpart can easily go up into a rear.

Here are some firsthand accounts of my experiences with rearing horses, finding the cause of the rear, and eliminating the behavior.

Lacy's story

Lacy was purchased by a middle aged woman who rode as a child and wanted to get back into horses after having taken some time away to raise her family. On a whim, she attended a horse auction and walked away with a grade (unregistered) Paint mare about which she knew little to nothing, other than that a small boy had ridden her in a round pen with nothing but a halter and lead rope. Having witnessed this, she was certain it must be a wonderfully calm mare and she bought her for $500. She proceeded to go out and buy a beautiful matching bridle and saddle set, headed out to the barn where she had decided to board Lacy, and got on. The moment she picked up the slightest amount on the reins, Lacy reared straight up. The woman tried several times to ride the mare by herself, with the same end result. Any bit contact resulted in rearing. Scared and confused, she called several trainers, including myself, and I agreed to take her mare in training.

Lacy arrived the next week and was a very quiet, pretty mare with excellent ground manners and a kind eye. As always, I looked for a physical problem first. With rearing, especially provoked by bit pressure, the culprit is almost always the teeth, even when using the mildest of bits, which was the case with Lacy.

For those not familiar with dental work in horses, it is necessary to have maintenance work done to ensure even wearing of the teeth. Unlike humans, horses' teeth continue to grow throughout their lives, and need to be "floated" by filing down points that develop and maintaining a flat grinding surface for effective chewing. Irregular wearing can cause problems in the mouth. Dental issues can cause the horse to have difficulty eating, as well as problems with bridling and riding.

I recommend checking in the spring and fall to watch for problems and have a maintenance float done once a year, more often if necessary as problems can arise easily. A basic dental exam can be done by quietly grasping the horse's tongue and sliding it to the side and out of the mouth so it is between the upper and lower teeth. In this manner, you can safely slide your other hand along the sides of the teeth and feel for points or other problems horses can develop, while the tongue prevents the horse from biting down on your hand. A secondary person can hold a flashlight and also get a limited look at the tongue and cheeks. Horses are not always cooperative about this and it takes practice to accomplish quietly, so do not attempt this on your own, at least at first.

Even with this brief exam, I could tell Lacy's teeth had not been done in a long time, if ever. The poor mare had numerous points and hooks on both sides of her mouth, and extensive ulcers inside her cheeks and damage on her tongue from the neglected teeth. We scheduled a vet appointment as soon as possible to get her mouth taken care of. After her teeth were floated, we gave her two weeks off to let her mouth heal before putting her to work.

Confident her mouth was healed, but not knowing her riding history, I put her through my program for starting a horse under saddle. Lacy knew her basics quite well and I started putting a plain snaffle bit in her mouth to let her get accustomed to a the bit being there without the pain. After a few days of this, I slowly started applying gentle pressure on the bit when moving forward. Not unexpectedly, Lacy responded by rearing when the bit pressure was applied. Staying quiet and consistent, I maintained the pressure and allowed Lacy to realize there was no longer pain associated with bit pressure. Over the next few days Lacy realized there was no pain, and she relaxed into the training program with the quiet temperament she had always exhibited in other areas. Lacy was with me for three months and evolved into a reliable trail riding horse for her very relieved owner.

As mentioned in the bucking chapter, a physical cause can turn into a behavioral problem if the horse makes the mental connection between the evasive behavior and getting out of work/exercise. In these cases the rearing needs to be treated as a behavioral response, which we will cover next. Thankfully Lacy had not made this connection and we were able to proceed with her training right away.

Dexter's story

"Don't buy pretty, buy functional, and if they're pretty too you got it made!" I had a farrier (the professional who trims and shoes the horse's hooves) who used to say this to all the starry eyed young girls looking for that magical first horse. Beauty has a tendency to blur common sense when it comes to life, and horses are no exception. We're all guilty of it and sometimes it comes back to bite us, as was the case with Dexter, a big and drop dead gorgeous paint gelding. I can remember the excitement in the woman's voice as she described to me how beautiful her newest acquisition was. "But how does he ride?" I asked.....I would soon find out.

Dexter had been started under saddle to ride, but appeared to be very green, so we proceeded slowly. As with Lacy, his ground manners and ground work were all satisfactory. My first ride on Dexter was going quite well as I went through and checked all the basics green horses should know before progressing. That is, until the other horse being worked in the arena left. Dexter got very agitated, calling to the other horse and pawing. I redirected his attention and worked on getting him focused back on me, at which point he reared straight up....and stayed there. I could feel the saddle sliding back slightly as he stood on his back legs for an impressive amount of time. I have worked with and ridden a lot of rears in my time, but I have to admit the grace and balance with which he reared seemed to show evidence of quite a bit of practice. As most horse professionals will agree, a horse doesn't just one day go all the way up in a rear and remain balanced and confident without having worked up to that point. It was apparent that Dexter had a good bit of experience in the rearing department before my client bought him. He was now her problem, making him my newest project.

Again, rearing, especially full-height rearing, is quite dangerous for horse and rider, so we started from scratch with this gelding. I had already made sure tack fit was correct, but did one more quick physical check just to make sure I was accurate in assessing this as behavioral, not physical. Everything was fine physically so we moved on. I went back to ground driving Dexter and reintroduced the last trigger – a horse leaving the arena. As anticipated, he was doing fine until the horse left, but then escalated quickly into the rear. Addressing this from the ground is much safer, and I sent him forward and aggressively put him to work verbally disciplining the behavior and incorporating a supportive physical cue, tapping on his hindquarters with the whip to reinforce the forward cues.

The key in discouraging rearing is forward movement. Keep the feet moving and the horse cannot shift its weight back to rear. Dexter was an expert at ignoring the forward cue and shifting his weight to pull off the rear, so I had to step it up a notch. I strengthened the forward cue and disciplined the rear in increasing levels until he would go forward. It was obvious by his escalating negative behavior that he was used to people being intimidated and backing off when he reared in the past. It was also quickly evident that rearing was his go-to move whenever he was at all displeased with his current situation.

He was so frustrated at his inability to make me leave him alone by rearing up that he resorted to temper tantrums. At one point, we were ground driving down the rail of the indoor arena and he got agitated and started rearing, which reliably got him disciplined and the demand to go forward, so he literally threw himself on the ground as he was coming down from the rear. He hesitated a moment, got up and I sent him forward again. We maintained this consistent path of training until he had not reared for a full week when on the ground lines. He had learned to control his behavior and focus on the work he was being asked to do, and was starting to see that rearing was no longer paying off. We were ready to move on to riding.

At this point I had gotten to know Dexter pretty well, so I was confident we could get him going under saddle with little to no relapse in the rearing. Every horse gives signals when they are uncomfortable and thinking of performing a past negative habit.

When we pay attention and recognize these signals, we have an opportunity to intervene before the behavior occurs. Dexter would bob his head and start to paw when he was starting to think about rearing. All I had to do was pay attention and get his feet moving when he started this behavior and things went smoothly. He already learned that rearing would be verbally and physically disciplined, and he would be asked to work even harder after a rear, so it was easy for him to understand that the same protocol applied when he was being ridden.

I am happy to report that Dexter is still owned by the same person and is a very well behaved horse. She often rides him bareback in a halter and lead rope, and he respects her and responds very well.

The training protocol used with Dexter to curb a very well developed rearing behavior should only be done by an experienced horseperson or a trainer that is familiar with this behavior and well versed in ground driving and behavior modification. It is not to be tried by the everyday horse owner. Dexter is just an example of rearing that stems from a behavioral response by the horse. He is also a good example of how our allowing, or inadvertently rewarding, a negative behavior can escalate into something quite dangerous.

Nickel's story

Nickel was a grey gelding that rode well in a smooth snaffle but had a history of rearing with any sort of leverage bit (meaning one that applies pressure to the poll and chin, not just the corners of the mouth) when at his previous trainer's facility. His owner had left that facility to move to a boarding stable where there were more people to ride with. She decided she wanted to start showing Nickel in western pleasure. She approached me to help her teach him to neck rein and accept a bit with a shank, as he was over five years old and rules and regulations for showing state that horses six years and over must be ridden one-handed with a legal western bit. Horses five years and under can be ridden two handed in a snaffle or a bosal.

She did inform me that, with the previous trainer, he would rear when ridden in a bit with a shank. She had been told by that trainer that the horse would never accept being ridden in a shank. I started working with Nickel, first using a snaffle to make sure he was ready to move forward with his training. He worked well, learned quickly, and was soon ready to move up to a shank.

Where bits are concerned, I believe that less is more, so I started with the mildest shank possible. Nickel's response was one of fear and intimidation. With the slightest movement of my hand he would flinch and refuse to go forward, immediately getting light in the front end. He showed telltale signs that he had been mishandled in a shank. Somebody had pulled hard on his face and he had become fearful of the leverage pressures of a shank bit. This is not uncommon as people tend to put in too much of a bit too soon, and also use their hands too heavily. The bridle and bit should be used as a gentle guide and collection tool. A properly trained horse should respond to seat, leg, and breathing, not just pressure through the bridle.

Nickel's reaction was an emotional response (fear of pain) and needed to be treated as such. His fear was overpowering him and we needed to break through that barrier. He was anticipating the worst, so I had to convince him that this was not going to be the same as his experience with a shank in the past. I started just moving his feet around while applying minimal pressure to the bridle, staying soft in my hands and encouraging movement with my seat and leg. At no time did I increase the bit pressure to more than minimal at this point. When he started accepting that, we moved on to more regulated steering and transition work with minimal bit pressure, focusing on response to seat and leg. Whenever he became agitated I just kept his feet moving until he relaxed again.

As he progressed over the next few weeks, he started to allow me to pick up on the reins and the bit more and more, to lift his shoulders and round him under the saddle without fearing the bit contact. We proceeded this way, slowly introducing more bit pressure until he was responding quietly and was relaxed at all times.

Nickel became a successful western pleasure horse for his owner. She also had to practice to become soft and consistent with her hands, as horses can relapse easily if put in stressful situations that remind them of past fear or pain. A horse that has been mishandled in the bridle is more reactive to too much bit pressure than a horse that has not had those negative experiences, with some individuals being more sensitive than others. Previous mistreatment can leave scars. The wounds can be healed but the horse does not forget. These horses must be handled with care, and with consideration of their past difficulties.

Rearing is a negative behavior that is best handled by a professional. There are many different causes, levels of severity, and ways to alter this behavior. It is by far the most dangerous negative behavior a horse can exhibit and must be viewed as such by the recreational horse owner. I recommend addressing this issue as soon as you notice signs of the behavior, for the safety of everyone involved – horse and human.

CHAPTER 5
BOLTING

"The wind of heaven is that which blows between a horse's ears."
~Arabian proverb

Bolting is best described as a horse going at a faster pace than the handler/rider wants, while refusing to listen to cues to slow down or stop. When being handled from the ground, the horse will use its body weight to push into the headstall, run past the handler, and go forward, and the handler is either dragged or lets go of the horse. When being ridden, the horse will usually "run off" with the rider, again ignoring any slowdown/halt cues the rider may attempt.

Usually, a horse will stop when its reason for bolting is removed. If it is running back to the barn, it will stop when it gets there. If it is running from a spook, it will stop when the fear, real or imagined, is far enough away, etc. Most horses will bolt at some time in their life. Remembering the basics from early chapters, this is decidedly normal prey behavior. Whether it's a loud noise from behind, excess energy from a lack of exercise, or any other of a wide array of circumstances, there will likely come a time when your horse exhibits this behavior. It's usually a short-lived and unusual reaction, and you and your horse can go on with your lives without much concern.

The problem arises when it becomes a habit for the horse, and it reacts by routinely bolting when a certain set of circumstances arises. When this behavioral trend emerges, action must be taken to curb the behavior. A horse running without regard for its handler/rider can be extremely dangerous to itself, the person handling the horse, and any surrounding people, horses and /or structures.

Versaci's story

Versaci was a finished show horse, experienced in showmanship, hunt seat and western pleasure, equitation and horsemanship, and trail. He was shown at open and breed shows quite successfully by a teenage girl who loved him to no end. I had personally worked with this horse on and off as needed, and I also admired his athleticism and sweet personality.

Problems started one summer in the middle of the show season. The family had gone to a show, and when they returned they relayed the story of how in the middle of a hunt seat pleasure class, while cantering, Versaci had thrown his head and taken off with his rider. She asked him to stop several times without luck, and when he finally ran towards the rail and turned suddenly, she had come off the horse. The horse had never exhibited this behavior before, and after dusting herself off and remounting Versaci was good as gold the rest of the day. Chalking it up to a very out-of-character spook, we thought nothing of it and continued lessons and riding as usual.

Several weeks later, when I happened to be away from the barn running errands, I received a phone call that Versaci had again exhibited the same head toss and bolting behavior as at the show weeks ago. Again he ran at the fence and turned, causing his rider to fall off. The girl's mother wanted me to ride the horse the next day to see if I could determine the cause of his behavior. I of course agreed, as it was disturbing that he had done this same behavior again.

I rode Versaci the next day and he was an absolute angel, no sign of the trouble he had given his rider the previous day. The next step was to set up a lesson and observe his rider and Versaci closely to try and figure out the cause. Again, it was a completely uneventful ride, with Versaci being an absolute dream. I backtracked and checked teeth, tack, for back soreness, everything checked out fine. Stumped, but finding nothing wrong with the horse or the tack, I simply suggested she ride him in correlation to my schedule so I could observe them while I was riding and giving other lessons.

Five days later, I was able to witness one of Versaci's episodes. He went from cantering quietly down the rail to a head toss and bolting. I was able to talk his rider through getting his head pulled around and disengaging his hip to get him stopped without her coming off this time. This time I had a valuable piece of information: when Versaci tossed his head I was able to observe his body language, and more importantly his facial expression. His eyes were panicked; something was upsetting him enough to get this violent of a reaction out of a normally quiet well-behaved horse. My other clue was that he had only ever exhibited this behavior during a right lead canter. We dug in; I got on him and put him through his paces. Bending, flexing, transitions, heavy collection, light collection, we did it all. I noticed he had a hard time holding his lead in the back when circling right on heavier inside bend and collection. Several times he tried unsuccessfully to take the bit from me when asked to perform this maneuver. After about 45 minutes of detailed working I had a pretty good idea of Versaci's problem. He had some sort of pain/discomfort stemming from his back end during the right lead canter that seemed to be exacerbated when asked for more bend and collection. His body language was clear, this was uncomfortable for him.

The next step was to get a vet out to do an evaluation. During the flexion test, where each leg is held up one at a time and each joint is flexed individually, it became apparent that he was sore in his left stifle. The left hind is the drive leg for the right lead, and when he needed to increase the physical demand on that leg by stepping underneath himself more and driving better, he was having significant pain.

After discussing his recent behavior and the findings of the vet that day, we deduced that he was throwing his head and bolting when he would get a more intense pain stemming from his left stifle. Further diagnostics revealed some mild arthritis and inflammation in that joint. This was nothing too serious, so Versaci was put on six weeks stall rest and given anti-inflammatory medication for one week, to give the joint time to heal.

When rechecked six weeks later, the joint was looking much better and he was started on a rehabilitation program to get him back to work. It was also decided to put him on a joint supplement to help with the mild arthritis. Several weeks went by and Versaci was doing great. Confident that we had the problem taken care of, Versaci went back to normal work and showing.

The hardest part about Versaci's behavioral issue was being able to see the whole picture and get the small, subtle clues. My biggest revelation came when I was able to see Versaci's eyes during an episode. If you're around horses long enough, you will eventually see the look of fear/pain/panic in a horse's eyes. It's haunting and unforgettable. The other strong indicator was that, while it seemed to be inconsistent behavior, in actuality it was always during a right lead canter. Once we recognized that element, we were able to identify and remedy the physical difficulty Versaci was having.

Fortunately, this behavior had not gone on long enough to persist as a negative behavioral issue once the source had been eliminated. This is not always the case. If he had done this a few more times, resulting in his rider coming off, it could easily have turned into an ongoing issue even after the initial physical cause was removed. Then it would need to be treated as a purely behavioral issued and treated, disciplined as such.

Black's story

Up until now we have looked at these negative behaviors under saddle; this isn't the case with Black. Black was a very tall, confident, gelding and was only a year and a half old when I met him. Too young to start under saddle, his owner had started him on some ground work to establish a foundation to move forward from once he was physically mature enough to start his riding career. She had her own place, and several other horses that she had enlisted my help with in the past for various tune-ups and progression work, but this was her first youngster.

At first, all was going well and his in-hand work was coming along nicely. As I mentioned he was a very confident leggy boy and a little pushy when he felt like it, which was usually curbed with mild discipline. One day he was feeling especially uncooperative and decided he would rather be turned out with the other horses than work on ground manners. He pushed past his owner and out the barn door, pulling the lead rope out of her hand and running off into the paddock with his buddies. This resulted in all of them running laps in the paddock, Black with his lead rope flying behind, for quite a length of time. When she finally caught him and took him back into the barn he was winded and sweaty and feeling much more cooperative. She proceeded to run him through his ground work and put him away.

The next day – you guessed it – as soon as she brought him into the barn he took his head, whipped around, and went running back out into the paddock with his friends. Again, after a long bout of running he was caught, worked, and put away. That night she called me, realizing this was going to become an ongoing problem. I couldn't get out to her place for a few days, so I had her leave him in his stall the next day when the other horses were turned out. I told her to close the barn door access to the turnout area and take him into a different paddock enclosure, completely separate from any access to the other horses. This worked for a short time, but then Black decided even if he couldn't get to his buddies, he could still run around and have some fun. He pulled back, whipped around, and took off, lead rope flapping, doing laps up and down the fence line. She decided to try a few more times before I could make it out to her place; her pride was wounded, and she couldn't bear to just sit and wait for me to get out there. This only made things worse as he was taking off on her sooner and sooner into their ground work sessions. She tried both a chain and rope halter with no success. Black was making a choice to get away from his handler to have his own fun. He had learned that he could, so now we needed to change his mind.

I made it out to her place that weekend and she tearfully filled me in on his increasingly negative behavior. I had her bring him out so I could see what was going on. She attempted to just lead him around the paddock and, within several minutes, he flew past her, ripping the rope from her hand and happily running laps on his own. There appeared to be nothing present other than sheer enjoyment of his new-found game. There was no other apparent stimulus, pain, or fear, just his desire to do his own thing.

We made the work enclosure smaller By running some fence through the middle of it, giving me the advantage keeping him close enough to stay in control of his movement when he was running loose. Here was the plan to thwart his new found fun: turn it into work. I led him into the enclosure and, when he made his move to get away, I appealed to the existing ground work training that had been done, asking him to stay controlled and with me. When he chose to take off anyway, I took control of his movement. Using a lunge whip, I kept cutting him off, turning him, and driving him forward. He slowly started to realize he was not in control, and as he grew tired and wanted to slow down and stop I kept pushing him to keep going. We could see him decide that this was no longer fun!

After pushing him longer than he would have liked to keep going, I allowed him to stop. I resumed control of him with his halter and lead, and finished the ground work session. I increased his ground work skills, getting him to yield much better to pressure, to pay closer attention to his handler and to the body language and cues of the exercises he was being asked to do. I have an extensive list of requirements for horses to be able to manage in their groundwork; this increases body control of the horse and helps curb any mischief that might crop up. When a proper response is deeply ingrained through consistent training, so much a matter of muscle memory for horse and handler, training comes through in times where circumstances could easily spiral out of control.

I came out three times a week throughout the month, keeping with the same protocol. Black soon decided the behavior was no longer fun and became less interested in running off while being handled. I taught his owner how to run the disciplinary exercise when the behavior occurred and she kept with the process. Black is now a very well-behaved, polite trail horse. He just needed to be shown that taking off when being handled was not a good choice for him to make. It was much easier to just do what was being asked of him.

Blake's story

Blake was a showmanship machine, he had it down cold, and he could run a pattern with his handler without a halter and lead. He picked up on every movement as if he could read his owner's mind! It seemed that Blake loved the detailed precision of showmanship and had been trained very well in all the necessary elements.

Showmanship class, in the show world, consists of completing an in-hand pattern with your horse. They must walk, trot, halt, pivot, back, set-up all with very slight cues from the handler. When done well it's like a beautiful ballet, and Blake and his handler were unbeatable within their barn. That is, until the new horse came.

The girl's family had moved from another state and she brought her horse to the same barn Blake was at. Her horse was amazing, especially at showmanship. Blake's owner became insecure about another horse/handler combo being better than her and her superhorse. She became harsh with Blake; her calm, quiet confidence was replaced by an ugly insecurity. She kept pushing him to be better and better, no longer praising when he did well, over-disciplining for the slightest mistake, losing track of her love for her horse and showmanship, focusing only on winning the showmanship class at the next show. Her competition included the new girl and her horse, and they were good.

I could see the relationship between Blake and his owner disintegrating. Blake started pinning his ears, resisting, and then eventually he started to run away from his handler. He got to the point that whenever she would start to work on showmanship Blake would take off, sometimes knocking her over to get away. That's when her mother asked me to step in. I had seen what was going on and had a long talk with his young owner. We talked about reestablishing the trusting, loving relationship she had lost with Blake in her desire to maintain her position as best in the barn at showmanship. We started back slowly with Blake. She earned his trust back by rewarding his efforts and being a consistent partner to him.

Once trust has been broken between horse and human, it is a long road to getting it back. It is also never as strong as it was before the betrayal that destroyed it. While Blake and his owner improved, he maintained the defensive, tense body language when he was performing his showmanship patterns. He had learned to fear making a mistake and was always waiting for his handler to lose her temper and over-discipline him for the slightest misstep. It was heartbreaking for his owner and everyone who knew them. The answer? Stop showmanship for a while and work on trust-building exercises between Blake and his owner. The bolting or running away that had started to occur during the time period where he was being treated unfairly was not what needed to be fixed. The emotional damage that had occurred needed to be addressed. The remedy was to have some fun together.

One of the things I have found to be therapeutic for both horse and handler is trail riding: venturing out together and tackling obstacles and terrain, trotting and cantering through fields, quality time together. Blake's owner was to go on at least one long trail ride a week to just have fun together, rediscover the love for her horse and reconnect with him. After a few weeks we could see the relationship improving, Blake had softness in his eyes again. Now came the hard part, incorporating showmanship again.

We started with just basics for ten minutes after a trail ride. As that went well we slowly started increasing the amount of time and level of performance we were requiring of Blake in his showmanship work. We went with his comfort level, as his eyes stayed soft, we continued, if he started tensing up we did something different and fun. After several months Blake was back to showing in showmanship classes and winning. His owner learned a valuable lesson about patience and realistic goals for herself and her horse. Push too hard and too fast and disaster will ensue. Blake went the route of bolting when he got to his emotional breaking point, but that wasn't the problem to be solved, it was merely a symptom.

Bolting is a scary behavior because it gives the handler/rider a feeling of helplessness. Whether it's done out of pain, mischief, or self-preservation, feeling completely out of control of a massive animal, especially when you're along for the ride is intimidating to say the least. Keeping your horse in a controlled, enclosed environment until the behavior is curbed is of the utmost importance. Bolting is one of the behavioral issues that can not only harm the horse and handler involved, but also the people, horses, and property surrounding them, so you will want to eliminate that possibility of collateral damage from the equation. A good rider will also have an arsenal of techniques that can be called upon if this behavior occurs. A solid one-rein stop, an ingrained yielding of the hindquarters, maintaining a softness in the horses face, along with strong respect and trust can ensure that you will be able to safely and confidently handle a horse that may bolt.

CHAPTER 6
BITING

Show me your horses and I will tell you what you are."   *~English proverb*

Plain and simple, biting is when the horse's mouth opens to grasp something other than food between its teeth. For our purposes we will consider biting as anytime the lips open at all, whether to grab something with the teeth or with just the lips themselves. Biting is a frustrating behavior, as horse's are quick and it can be difficult to counter the behavior. Whether it's a simple grabbing of your jacket sleeve or an ears pinned, mouth open, lunge at your arm, biting is unacceptable. It is not cute, funny, or amusing to let them play with your jacket zipper or dig in your pockets for a treat. A horse can do significant damage with its teeth, even when you think it is just a playful nip.

There are some possible physical reasons for biting, although it is typically a behavioral issue. One of the most common is ulcers. Due to the abdominal discomfort of ulcers, a horse may exhibit a desire to bite when being groomed or saddled or when leg is applied to the horse under saddle. This is usually accompanied by teeth grinding and tail swishing. If you feel your horse may suffer from ulcers, consult your veterinarian about diagnosis and treatment.

Some mares become ultra-sensitive when they are in heat and can also be prone to biting when pressure is applied to their sides and hindquarters. There are certain drugs and supplements that can be given to minimize this reaction. Discipline and behavior modification can also be used successfully in these cases when the horse is being extremely aggressive.

Most often biting is a mischievous game or an aggressive tendency that has developed, and nine times out of ten the owner has initiated it, allowed it, or made it worse through inadequate or inconsistent discipline.

Plato's story

Plato was a three-year-old stallion being used for breeding purposes. He was 16.2 hands high and solid, beautiful, and strong. The owner wanted him to be started under saddle and shown lightly to increase his value and stud fee. I was told flat out that he had an aggressive biting habit, not a playful nip your jacket, but the "all-out, mouth open, ears pinned, and I'm going to take a chunk out of you" kind.

He was an overall confident and highly aggressive horse. He had learned to intimidate and bully people at the previous barn he was at. He would threaten, and if that did not deter you he would come at you with intent. You don't come across this level of confident aggression very often, and usually it is created by people, not a natural way of behaving for horses. Through speaking with his owner I discovered this to be true of Plato. As a foal and yearling he was a very sweet boy. He was not aggressive by nature. Someone had taught this horse to fight. I learned that the previous person they had hired to start him was not experienced in handling stallions and not confident enough to deal with the increasingly stallion-like dominance he developed as he matured. She would attempt to discipline him for his alpha behavior, but she was not experienced or confident enough and he was winning the battles.

When Plato came to me he was an egotistical, arrogant, pushy, rude, and overall aggressive horse. Whenever anyone did something he viewed as a threat to his leadership he would pin his ears and come at them. Even routine chores like cleaning his stall when he was in it became a constant power struggle. If asked to move over, he refused, and if the person insisted, he became aggressive. This is the type of behavior that immediately needs to be handed over to a trainer with a lot of confidence and experience, or someone is going to get hurt badly and the horse will continue to become more and more aggressive and dangerous.

As a side note, aggressive behavior issues are more common and pronounced in stallions, as the addition of testosterone to the equation makes the situation that much harder to deal with. In general, these aggressive tendencies are not as pronounced in mares and geldings.

The first thing I did was make it perfectly clear at the barn that no one was allowed to interact with Plato except for myself. No one was to clean his stall, turn him out, or handle him at all. It was too much of a risk and I also needed to make a clear impression on Plato that this behavior was never going to be allowed again. Allowing him the opportunity to get away with any negative behavior towards anyone else in the barn would slow my progress.

A horse that has been getting away with a behavior for an extended period of time, one that is used to being in control, is ten times harder to work with. They escalate before they reform. When Plato challenged me and I not only refused to yield to him but challenged him in return, he became extremely frustrated and escalated his threats and ultimately his attempts to physically influence me.

When working with horses like Plato, safety is a top priority. Staying out of striking range is key when working with them. A round pen is ideal, as you can work the horse, move its feet, and control its direction and speed from a safe distance.

Controlling their movement is the first step to establishing a respect relationship. The alpha horse in the herd controls the other horses' movement. They say when to move and how fast to move. I needed to establish this with Plato. The added problem with him was that he was confident enough to actually charge me when he did not want to cooperate with the round pen exercises. I needed to carry a riding crop and a lunge whip and challenge him back at these times. It takes an experienced and confident trainer to deter a horse effectively at these times. You need to convince the horse that you are willing to do what it takes to achieve and maintain an alpha position. Realistically, the horse is much stronger, faster, and capable of taking a person down if they truly want to; the key is not allowing them the opportunity to figure that out.

Plato slowly came around to respecting my authority in the round pen, and it was time to handle him at a closer distance. I still maintained the "no contact" rule with everyone else in the barn. The first day of closer contact work, Plato attempted to bite and threaten multiple times, all of which were met with stern discipline and a good session of moving his feet and making him work. Again, slowly, the aggressive threatening and biting subsided. Over weeks and then months of consistent and dedicated work, we continued to develop a strong, mutual respect relationship and he blossomed into a great horse under saddle. At his first show he won both his classes easily.

We had come to an understanding, but what about other people? Would he respect their authority? You never know how a horse is going to behave with others until you try. Some are willing to carry over their training and respect, and others will test and resist a new handler. Plato was the latter. He proceeded to test his owners, culminating in the need for them to take extensive lessons from me on how to discipline Plato's dominant tendencies and acquire his respect. Ultimately they decided he was better off with a trainer who could keep him in constant check, and sold him to a breeding and training facility where he continued his show career.

Plato was a case that was destined for a trainer's intervention. He truly would have continued his path of aggression and dominance and ultimately would have hurt many people. The sad part is that it wasn't his fault. If he had been handled correctly early on, he would not have developed the level of aggression that he had.

The moral of this particular story is to carefully check into the person with whom you are entrusting your horse, check in regularly, go see your horse and gauge their progress. Not everyone is capable of handling every situation, and it's perfectly acceptable to shop around and check references. A bad experience can significantly affect the behavior of a horse, so choose wisely and don't be hesitant to pull the plug if you're uncomfortable with the situation once you're in it.

Kit's story

Kit's story is one that echoes through every barn – the horse that begins to nip and get "mouthy" from being given treats from the hand. Here's Kit's scenario: his owner goes to his stall to get him and gives him a treat before she puts his halter on. She puts him in the crossties and begins grooming; he cranes his head around and gives her a look, so she produces another treat for her "sweet boy." She saddles him and, before she puts the bridle on, slips him another treat so he'll "like" being bridled. They enjoy a beautiful ride together and she dismounts to return him to the crossties. After removing his bridle he gets another treat to show him what a good boy he was. After removing the saddle and noticing he got a touch sweaty, she produces another treat from her bottomless pocket because she feels bad for "working him so hard." After he is untacked and groomed, she gives him another handful of treats before taking him back to his stall. Repeat this scenario on a weekly basis and what happens?

Fast forward one month. Kit's owner goes to get him from his stall and before she can get the treat from her pocket he is grabbing at her jacket, digging in her pocket already, eager for the now-expected treat. Laughing, she pushes his head away and gets the treat out and gives it to him, thinking how cute he looked rummaging around in her pockets. As they walk to the crossties Kit grabs her jacket pocket repeatedly demanding the next "I look so cute while you're brushing me treat" a little early. Again, his head is pushed away and crossties are put on and then, you got it, the treat is produced. This routine continues for another week.

Kit's owner is in a hurry today, she has an appointment and not much time so she forgot to bring the new bag of treats to the barn with her. Oh well, Kit will survive one day without his oral rewards for just being *the cutest, sweetest horse alive*! She goes to get him out of his stall and he pushes into her pockets for his treat, she pushes his head away *and does not produce a treat*!!! Frustrated, Kit pushes into her pocket again, harder. She pushes him away and attempts to lead him to the crossties while he is nudging her pockets and grabbing her sleeve trying to make his guaranteed treat appear. Frustrated with his behavior she actually disciplines him with a smack on the nose with the lead rope and to her horror he pins his ears and bites at her hand!! Confused and now a little scared, she steps back and attempts to discipline him again. He continues the ear pinning while she attaches the crossties and is grabbing at her jacket and sleeves every chance he gets. He turns his head side to side as she is grooming him, pawing the ground, and grabbing at the crossties with his mouth. Kit's owner is extremely distressed, what is wrong with her sweet boy! After she puts him away, she calls me.

If I had a dollar for every time this scenario happened, I would be a multimillionaire. I observe this incessant treat-giving behavior with so many well-intentioned people that I have the script down for breaking the news to them that they are the cause of their horse's behavior. Fortunately the answer is clear, stop giving those treats. If you must, put the treats in the grain bin in their stall for them to enjoy later but honestly, your horse does not need treats to survive. They need structure and respect and verbal praise and a good scratch on the neck for a job well done. Your horse will blossom from all of these things.

Unfortunately, even after stopping the treats, ridding the horse of the now-unwanted mouthy behavior that turned into frustrated biting is a little harder to do. Imagine taking your four-year-old child to the grocery store every Sunday and routinely allowing him to pick out a candy bar. Then one week you go to the store and are a little short on money so you tell him he cannot get a candy bar today. How do you anticipate he will react? Any way you look at it you will get a negative reaction from your child. It is unlikely that he will understand, and you are probably going to have a temper tantrum on your hands. Your child's personality and general demeanor will play a part in the severity, but it will likely occur. The same is true of horses; their core personality will help determine the level of temper tantrum they will have, but it is almost certain there will be one. The key is to be firm and consistent in not producing treats and incorporating discipline when your horse gets overly pushy and aggressive while you are implementing the new rule.

With Kit, I placed him in part-time training and made arrangements for his owner to be present at as many sessions as possible. As expected, he would search my body for treats and be firmly pushed away, told "quit," and then he would get mad. Kit would pin his ears and aggressively bite at my hand and arm. For this he would get a firm crack across the nose and/or neck with the end of the lead rope and again be told to "quit." I like the word "quit" as it is quick and easy to spit out firmly and does not resemble any other word that would be used as a verbal command. If Kit's behavior escalated, his punishment escalated. When he would stop the pushy behavior and stand quietly he would get a verbal reward and a scratch on the neck or chest. We continued this routine for the next month and the mouthy behavior declined. It was up to Kit's owner to continue the regimen, but for all intents and purposes the behavior was resolved.

People do not like to hear that a problem was caused by their own actions. We can get defensive and angry and try to make excuses, but the bottom line is that a mistake was made, and the horse was conditioned by the owner's actions to behave this way. This is why we must try to understand a horse's thought process and act accordingly. Evaluate what you are doing and try and think of the behavior you may be inadvertently promoting. (Recall the concepts explained in Chapters One and Two.) Achieving a better understanding of the horse's way of thinking can prevent these unnecessary situations from developing in the first place.

CHAPTER 7
KICKING AND STRIKING

"Of all creatures God made at the Creation, there is none more excellent, or so much to be respected, as a horse."   *~Bedouin*

Kicking can be described as a horse using one or both its hind legs to either threaten or actively inflict damage to an object, living or otherwise. Striking is when a horse uses one or both front legs to the same effect. Whether the horse is simply threatening or actually following through, the behavior is never acceptable when the horse is being worked with or handled in any way shape or form. Horses do also 'playfully' kick at or strike out at pasture mates, but it cannot be tolerated at all when interacting with people.

A horse's hooves can inflict massive damage to a person or object. We have all seen a playful kick/strike accidentally cause significant damage to pasture mates when the timing or aim is off. Imagine what that blow can do to a person, especially if the horse is serious about the target and intensity. A well placed kick can not only seriously injure or kill a person, the horse can be seriously injured when kicking or striking an object such as a wall, horse trailer, fence, etc.

Kicking or striking can occur when a pain/discomfort response is triggered, such as when we examine for lameness or injury, or during dental work. The horse may kick/strike out when you are working in the area of pain or discomfort, so use caution during these times.

Kicking and striking may also occur if the horse is made to feel threatened or defensive in certain situations. Cornering a horse to try and force it to accept something often results in the horse "busting" its way out of the perceived entrapment.

Avery's story

From what I was told, Avery was a playful, energetic, and sweet young gelding. I was not introduced to this side of him. The horse I met was an ear pinning, stall-bar charging, aggressive animal. Unable to explain his change in attitude, his owner finally called me when the stall cleaner at the stable where he lived was kicked and badly injured. He had been trying to clean around Avery while the horse was eating. The boy said that Avery had swung his butt to him, aimed, and fired, nailing him firmly in the thigh. I agreed to come evaluate Avery.

Upon arriving at the facility where Avery was being kept, my first project was to get a detailed history from his owner. She had bought Avery as a two-year-old, sending him directly to a trainer to start him under saddle. The trainer gave glowing reports, commending Avery's sweet personality and willingness to learn. The owner had gone to see him and also agreed he was doing well, no signs of a problem. After several months in training, they moved Avery to a boarding facility closer to their home to continue riding and enjoying him themselves.

The days following the move Avery did well, got along with his pasture mates and was riding well for his owner. She didn't see a change in Avery until the start of his second week at the new facility. He started to seem crabby, unhappy, and became stall aggressive, swinging his hindquarters to the stall door and threatening to kick anyone that entered. This culminated into the stall cleaner getting kicked and everyone becoming very intimidated by Avery.

Hearing the story, I was sure there was a trigger for Avery's newfound nastiness so I went to see this monster in his stall. As predicted Avery pinned his ears, charged the bars, and became highly agitated when I approached his stall. I took his halter and lead and opened the stall door. Avery retreated to the back of the stall, still pinning his ears. When I stepped into the stall he promptly turned his hindquarters to me and threatened a kick. As soon as he did this, from the doorway of the stall I swung the lead rope, from a safe distance, out of kicking range, and connected with his rump. Avery continued to threaten and I continued to get him across the rump with the rope. Finally Avery turned to face me and I verbally praised him and became quiet with the lead rope. When I attempted to approach him again he promptly turned his hindquarters, and I got him across the rump again. He turned around again, confused by the fact that I wouldn't go away and wasn't intimidated by him. This time when I approached him he allowed it and I slipped his halter on. The rest of the work went fairly well. It was obvious the horse had some very good foundation training, but he definitely wasn't a happy boy. His responses were sullen and slow, and he objected to most everything before he would follow through with the correct response.

One of the things I noticed right away was how thin he was. Not neglectfully so, but definitely not at a healthy weight. He was still a growing boy at two-and-a-half years old, but surely we could get more weight on him. I asked about the feeding program and was shocked to find out the small amount of grain and hay he was getting. He should have been getting twice the amount. The barn owner informed me that they feed all the horses the same, they do not allow for tailored feeding programs or any extra hay for any of the horses. I now had a very good idea of what was going on with Avery.

To test my theory I came out the next day shortly after Avery had gotten his allotted amount of hay and opened his stall door. His reaction was twice as violent as the day before when he had had no food in his stall. He not only threatened to kick but turned and fired immediately! This time he got the snap end of the lead rope across his hindquarters until he turned to face me. I then praised him for this response.

Regardless of why a horse may kick, the behavior must be disciplined consistently and quickly. When Avery fired at me he got the snap end of the lead, while when he had only threatened he got only the rope end of the lead. Punishment must escalate as the dangerous behavior does. Regardless, I had my answer. Avery was hungry. He was not receiving an appropriate amount of food for his growing and active body. He was constantly hungry and at feeding time became aggressively protective of his limited food.

After discussing the fact that he would have to be moved to a facility that would feed him the appropriate amount of grain and hay, we began to discuss further training with Avery to get him past the aggressive behavior he had developed. In all likelihood the behavior would not just disappear when his feed was increased and his hunger was gone. It rarely does. When a horse becomes food or stall aggressive it can become a difficult habit to break. Along with simply becoming a learned behavior, my theory is that once an animal – horse, dog, even human – knows consistent hunger, the fear of not having enough food never truly goes away, and the protectiveness and defensiveness remains.

Avery was moved to a boarding stable that fed according to the horses' needs. Avery gained some weight and his overall attitude improved, except in his stall. Using discipline when the negative behavior occurred and praise for the correct and pleasant behavior, I continued to work with Avery for two months. I was able to get him to the point of anyone being able to enter his stall at any time. He still occasionally pins his ears when you enter while he is eating, but a firm verbal correction changes his mind very quickly. At this time, years later, Avery is a very happy show horse for his owner and has reverted back to the playful, energetic, happy gelding that she had bought as a two year old.

Avery's story had a happy ending, but someone was injured and his psychological well-being was damaged simply because his basic dietary needs were far from met. His owner knew he was being fed but did not have the knowledge to know or even question if it was enough. She trusted the barn owner to know what he needed. If you are not comfortable with deciding on a correct feeding program for your horse, ask your vet. Tell them the horse's work load and have them evaluate weight and health and recommend a feeding regimen. Don't blindly trust the barn owner, your friend who's had horses "forever," or even your trainer. Be your horse's advocate, ask questions, check in, and make sure that they are being properly cared for. It can save you and your horse a lot of frustration and negative experiences.

Queen's story

I remember walking into the barn and hearing an ungodly squealing noise followed by loud banging and ultimately someone yelling words that are not meant for innocent ears. What was going on?! I was informed that this was the handiwork of Queen, one of the five horses I was hired to work with. This should be interesting.

I private contract out to different people and was hired to start five horses under saddle that were all being sold to a ranch out west for trail riding purposes. Now, I love starting horses under saddle; it's very rewarding, fun work for me. A horse is able to make huge amounts of progress so quickly when you start them correctly. I met all five horses that day and got a brief synopsis of their personalities. They were all happy, healthy, friendly souls, except for one – Queen. She was a 15-hand stocky mare that had an attitude like a rabid dog and was more talented with her back end then I had seen in a very long time, if ever!

I was given Queen's history. She was bred and raised on the

farm, same as the other four, but always had a mean streak in her. She would corner the other horses, squealing and kicking away at any given time. She also would turn her wrath on inanimate objects and, when given the opportunity, people. She had already injured two employees on the farm. When one had tried to bring in another horse, she was at the gate and wheeled around and nailed him good. When the other fellow was feeding hay, she spun around and nailed him as he was leaving her stall. Oh, and her kicking was always accompanied by an unnatural squealing that would give you goose bumps and turn your blood cold. This was going to be a challenge.

The other four horses were unbelievably easy to work with, as they had had proper handling since birth. That is what made Queen so interesting, they had done everything correctly from the start, but she persisted in being an aggressive kicker nearly all of her waking moments. I started Queen the same as any other horse and she fought me quite consistently for the first week. I carried a dressage whip at all times when handling her and I swear she must have had the toughest hind end in the state from being disciplined for attempting to kick almost every few minutes.

It was a challenge and a game to her, but I had the upper hand as Queen also enjoyed working. It engaged her mind and she would briefly forget about kicking while I was working her around the round pen and putting her through the required elements of starting a horse. We slowly came to an understanding and her kicking behavior subsided over the next few weeks. She even mellowed out with her pasture mates and in her stall. Not completely, but less and less kicking every day.

It was time to start riding her. I was fully prepared for Queen to give me a kicking and squealing session the first few rides, but she was fully prepared and at the point where we could start riding. The first time in the saddle was very quiet. As always, I got on and off numerous times from both sides, from the ground and a mounting block. Queen was interested but relaxed and I believe quite bored with me!

Then I asked her to go forward. She took one step, became agitated and started backing up quickly, kicking and squealing like a banshee! Here it was – the temper tantrum we had to get through. I reinforced my forward commands with increasing firmness. She had these down cold through all of our ground work and ground driving exercises. I even used the end of the reins across her butt as reinforcement, but she kept going. We went backwards around that round pen at least five times, kicking and squealing, before she stopped to think.

I asked her again to go forward. This time we went five steps before the crazy squealing demon came out again, but this time it was only for two laps. We progressed this way for the next twenty minutes until she finally went forward quietly with no attempts to kick out.

We progressed this way for a few days until Queen decided it was much easier and much more fun to just go forward and focus on her work. I had grown to like and even admire this unusually quirky mare. Even though I liked her, I had no delusions that she was going to be suitable as a trail riding horse for the average rider. She was a hardcore alpha and always would be. She needed a home where her attitude could be kept in check on a daily basis. She was put together well and was an athletic, pretty mover. Queen was smart, too smart, and needed an advanced and experienced owner. I convinced her owner to let me find her a suitable home. Queen is now owned by an advanced rider who works closely with a trainer and shows her at open shows in hunt seat pleasure and hunter hack. I am told she still lets out an ungodly squeal and kick on occasion, but it is very infrequent and is handled properly and quickly.

Horses have just as wide an array of personalities as people do, and once in a while you get one that has been handled properly, has had no negative experiences, but still has an undesirable bad habit or personality trait that needs to be addressed. Queen apparently made the choice to behave the way she did for no reason other than she enjoyed it. It made her feel powerful and gave her an outlet for her naturally dominant and aggressive personality. She needed to be taught that her behavior was not acceptable when she was being handled and/or worked with in any way. When redirected into an activity she found fun and stimulating, the behavior subsided quite a bit on its own. Queen's natural tendencies and personality made her unsuitable for most of the general population to own and work with, but she and other horses like her do have a place in this world. They can become amazing athletes and dedicated partners when handled correctly.

Peaches' story

Many years ago at a behavioral clinic I was teaching, I met Peaches and her owner. He had submitted to be a participant in the clinic and sent me his information. He had owned Peaches for less than six months and was currently terrified of her. He had purchased a well-trained trail horse, as he was a beginner, and according to him she had promptly turned into a monster. He claimed that whenever he tried to handle her she would strike at him with her front hooves – sometimes one, sometimes both – until he would back away from her. He had gotten to the point where he was afraid to handle her at all.

Peaches came to the behavioral clinic. She was a pretty chestnut with a flaxen mane and tail and a sweet face. I unloaded her from the trailer, as her owner was too nervous. I took her into the arena and began checking her out. I put her through every ground work exercise possible and not once did she attempt to strike at me. She never pinned her ears or even tensed up for a moment. She was very well trained and, for me, behaved like an angel.

I handed her lead rope to her owner to observe what would happen. I asked him to put her through some of the most basic ground work to see what would occur. Not even five seconds after he took the lead rope the mare rocked back on her hindquarters and her front feet came off the ground. Observing her body language was invaluable at this point. Peaches had no intention of hurting the man. There was no ear pinning, no aggressiveness, and her body and eyes were quiet. She was actually very careful about her movements and, while she was extending her legs in what could have been considered a "striking" manner, not once did her hooves come near her owner. Now switch to observing her owner. When Peaches went up, he stepped backwards quickly and Peaches followed, coming off the ground again. Her owner stepped back again and she followed.

The auditors of the clinic erupted in laughter. This mare was herding her owner around the arena. Very gently and very effectively she was in essence "dancing" with him! This was no more than an inappropriate game to Peaches, and while it was not acceptable and could be dangerous, her demeanor was not aggressive or malicious. Peaches was simply playing. After I explained this to her owner and pointed out the key clues in her body language, he was relieved. We still had to curb the behavior, as it was highly inappropriate and dangerous; but it was clear his horse was not a "monster"!

How Peaches picked up on this little game we will never know, but we had to discourage it. With some coaching her owner learned to verbally and, with the rope halter, lead rope and a dressage whip, physically discipline the behavior. It didn't take much. As soon as Peaches discovered her owner no longer enjoyed this game or wanted her to behave this way, she stopped very quickly. It only took a few bumps on the halter and taps with the dressage whip to deter her.

Other than being slightly embarrassed, her owner was thrilled! Here he thought she had turned into a monster when she was only playing with him. She was still the sweet and well-mannered mare he had bought and they had a very bright future together. Just as a negative and aggressive behavior can be overlooked as playful and become a problem, a playful and, in the horses mind, innocent behavior can label the horse as dangerous and aggressive. When in doubt contact a professional to help evaluate what is going on with you and your horse!

Kicking and/or striking can be a very intimidating and dangerous behavior. A horse's hoof is extremely hard and unforgiving and the power that these animals can exert may seriously injure or kill a person. Even a mild kick by a horse's standard can be devastating to us.

I was once lifted off the ground and sent flying by the hind foot of a Percheron, and had to be carried out of the barn. I got lucky with only a deep tissue bruise to my thigh, but it could have ended much differently. I wasn't working with the horse but had passed behind him in the barn aisle without enough caution. We occasionally have to be put in our place and reminded to always be aware of our surroundings, especially near horses we may or may not be familiar with. I remember being impressed by that gelding's ability to send me flying with what was on his part a very halfhearted effort. We need to always respect the sheer power of these magnificent animals and conduct ourselves accordingly.

CHAPTER 8
EXTREME SPOOKING

"You can never rely on a horse that is educated by fear! There will always be something that he fears more than you. But when he trusts you, he will ask you what to do when he is afraid." ~Antoine de Pluvinel

Spooking can be described as when a horse reacts to an intimidating or perceived "scary" object, situation, and /or noise. Horses are by nature flight animals, meaning they will choose to try and leave a situation when they feel uncomfortable or stressed in any way. The problem arises when this natural instinctive reaction occurs while we are working or handling the animal.

Ideally we want the horse to react reasonably in these situations, and this can certainly be a trained response. Most horses can be taught to "spook" in a reasonable way and without an overly dramatic physical reaction. We cannot realistically ask the horse to not react at all, that is an unattainable goal. What we can do is discourage "overreacting" to stressful situations. Some horses react violently enough when spooking that it interferes with their work and can result in the rider or handler being injured. Reactions such as rearing and spinning, bolting, and jumping or running sideways are just some of the reactions we want to curb into a more reasonable display.

Some horses also become habitual spookers, meaning they intentionally find things to react to or even react to nothing at all. This usually occurs in horses that are bored with their work or have found out they can redirect the work through the "spooking game."

Whenever we have a situation where a horse spooking has become a serious concern for the owner, the first step is, as with all the other behaviors we have discussed, to find the reason for the behavior. Is it simply a case of needing to build a nervous horse's confidence in their handler and teach them to react more reasonably? Do we have a case of extreme boredom and need to stimulate and challenge the horse more? Do we have a horse that has learned to play the "spooking game" because they find it more fun than the work at hand and that it distracts their owner enough to redirect the whole session into just getting the horse "over it"? The cause has to be determined to successfully deter the behavior.

Lexi's story

Lexi was a two-year-old that had come to me for routine starting under saddle. She was a curious but confident mare, progressed easily through her groundwork and was under saddle in no time. I had no issues with her except for one. Lexi was incredibly athletic and she displayed one athletic feat on a regular basis. She could drop down and then run sideways at lightning speed whenever the mood struck. She was not a nervous horse, but she took advantage of any unusual sight or sound to show off her skill.

Now I have to say I have a pretty good seat that comes from riding all makes and models of horses daily for many years, but this little girl put my seat to the test. She would take advantage of any moment she felt I was the least bit distracted and would drop down several inches underneath me and run sideways at a speed that was more than impressive. She always picked a sight or sound to go along with this maneuver so it did present as actual spooking to the untrained eye, but it was definitely nothing more than a mischievous game. And she was good at it! However, because she was meant to be a trail horse and not a cutting horse, the behavior had to be discouraged.

When discouraging a behavior that outwardly presents as spooking, the key is to focus on the job you are asking the horse to do and discipline a deviation from the work itself, not the actual spook. For instance, if I was asking Lexi to circle left at a jog on inside bend and she decided to drop down and run right, I would discipline the fact that she was going against what I was asking her to do, not the action itself. In this scenario, I would discipline the lack of forward motion and the fact that Lexi was ignoring my seat, leg, and rein cues to circle left. If I were to focus on just Lexi's actions and lose sight of what we had been working on, Lexi would view that as a successful evasion. She would have gotten out of the task she had been doing via her "duck down and run right" method. This is the case with most horses that are not spooking out of actual fear or nervousness. They learn to manipulate the situation so that they are in control of their workouts. Whether the horse is doing it for fun, as in Lexi's case, or out of a lack of interest in performing a certain task, it is treated and resolved the same way.

After many failed attempts to deviate from the work at hand, and many experiences of firm discipline in the appropriate manner and redirection back to the work at hand, Lexi's behavior subsided. The question remains though, what to do when simply out on a relaxing trail ride with Lexi and she pulls her athletic stunt? The answer to this is simple: make the behavior completely unproductive. If Lexi ran right, I would firmly run her back to the left, putting her right back where she started. Keeping her occupied with changes in speed within gaits, serpentines when possible, lateral work, haunches in, etc., all would help to discourage the behavior and keep her on track.

Murray's story

For those of you who have not witnessed a horse reacting out of pure fear and panic, it is a sight not easily forgotten. This was the case with Murray; he was genuinely terrified of everything. The slightest shadow, the smallest noise, the very hint of something foreign to him and he would have a meltdown. Murray was broke to ride but was not ridden very often, as it was a constant struggle to keep him remotely focused due to his lack of confidence. His spooking was violent and, according to his owner, uncontrollable. She was sending him to me because her teenage daughter had shown a great interest in riding, but she did not feel Murray was the safe horse she thought she had purchased. She wanted to know if I could "fix" Murray and, if not, could I find a home for him.

Murray had been purchased through an auction, where according to his current owner he was extremely quiet. After she brought Murray home, he became a different horse. She was certain he must have been drugged at the auction, as he became a nervous wreck within a few days after. This was six months ago and she had only attempted to ride him a handful of times, all of which ended poorly. Anything would set him off, from a candy wrapper to a bird fluttering across the arena. A loud truck passing by or a sneeze or cough from his rider would send him into a panic attack. To make matters worse, he had no consistent reaction that he would go to. Most horses stick to a general pattern when they spook, a predictable maneuver, such as a rear and spin, running sideways or backwards, etc. Murray would vary between any combination of these.

The first step was to establish a connection with Murray. Through extensive round pen work and a technique called "joining up," I was able to get a fair amount of trust from the horse. Step two was to implement relaxation and control exercises that would be ingrained in Murray's brain as muscle memory reactions that would theoretically override his panic attacks. These exercises must be done frequently enough that the correct response from the horse becomes immediate and without resistance.

The first exercise is yielding to pressure. Whether it is halter pressure or pressure from a hand or leg, the horse must yield to it completely and totally. This plays an important part in yielding the jaw and hindquarters for our "emergency brake" to be installed. Sometimes called a "one rein stop," the emergency brake gives us control of the horse's body while we relax their mind and bring them back to us mentally. To start this process I use a well fitted rope halter and long lead. I stood next to Murray, halfway down his ribcage, facing his head. Placing my inside arm over his back I apply light pressure to the halter until he yields his head, completely resistance free, around to where I am standing. I repeated this process numerous times until Murray would bring his head around immediately after light pressure was applied.

We then moved to yielding his hindquarters. I stood next to Murray facing his hip. While applying light halter pressure, which he immediately would yield to, I applied pressure from my hand slightly behind where my leg would be positioned if I was riding him. The correct response is to step away from my hand, while remaining soft in the halter, by crossing the inside hind leg (closest to me) in front of the outside leg (farthest away from me). Again, I repeated this exercise until Murray would step away correctly and immediately every time pressure was applied.

It is important that the horse stay soft and yielding in the face and cross over correctly in the back to achieve a successful emergency brake to use during times of distress. We then graduated to achieving this yield while Murray wore the saddle and bridle in which he would be ridden. When this was complete and correct, Murray was ready to tackle the under saddle portion.

While on Murray's back, I applied the same face pressure as on the ground and, after he yielded successfully, I slid my leg back to where my hand was positioned when on the ground and ask him to yield his hindquarters. Repeating this process hundreds of times over the following weeks resulted in an immediate, muscle memory response on Murray's behalf. We then needed to implement this control at the walk, trot, and canter to ensure it would be there when we needed it during one of Murray's panic attacks. I require this process of all my horses, but it becomes even more imperative in a horse that will need it to remain safe and under control.

We then needed to build Murray's confidence in himself and his rider. After making sure all of his foundation work was solid, I moved on to adding certain stressors, in a controlled environment, to his workouts. I added these stressors during groundwork first, and then moved on to under saddle. I started small – recorded small noises, unnatural items in the arena, unanticipated rider noises and movements such as coughing, sneezing, rocking in the saddle, unzipping a sweatshirt, you get the idea. As expected, Murray would react violently and I would yield his head and neck until he quieted down and then put him immediately back to work. Soon Murray was reacting less, and more reasonably, to the stressors. He was beginning to understand that nothing bad was going to happen to him and he could trust his rider.

It was time to add bigger stressors into the equation – tarps, plastic bags, louder, more unusual recorded noises, riding with other horses, dogs, cats in the arena, etc. The same process followed, except for the fact that Murray started by reacting more reasonably right away. I still had to yield him around, but it became an easier and more quickly resolved episode with each occurrence. It was time to go outside.

After several weeks of new experiences and consistent responses on my part and on Murray's, he was ready to have his owner start riding him and learn how to control his ever-dwindling panic episodes. His yielding had been immediate and completely effective for weeks now. We started back in the controlled small environment, with me purposefully adding stressors that might get a reaction from Murray. To my satisfaction, Murray had very few meltdowns and his rider was able to handle each of them successfully. They were now building a trusting relationship with each other. Increasing their adventures to trail riding and showing, Murray was now a more confidant horse and his rider was also confidant in her ability to handle Murray if he did have an episode of fear or anxiety.

Real fear and insecurity needs to be handled with the utmost compassion and consistency. Gradual desensitization to sounds, sights, and unusual circumstances can improve your horse's ability to handle itself. You do not need to desensitize your horse to anything they might possibly come across that may cause it distress; you simply need to build its trust and confidence in itself and in you. Once it has self-confidence and has been taught how to react appropriately in stressful situations, the two of you are capable of tackling anything you come across.

Xena's story

How many of you have an actual phobia? Heights, swimming, spiders, big dogs – your heart pounds, your hands get sweaty, your respiration rate increases, and you just can't get over it no matter how much you want to or try. Horses can also have phobias, debilitating, and insurmountable fear of an object or noise. Xena was one of those cases.

Xena was an amazing mare who did hunt seat, western, jumping, driving, trail class, and trail riding. Pretty much everything you asked of her she would take on willingly and become good at it in a short amount of time. I had worked with this mare and her owner a lot and there was nothing they couldn't accomplish. Until the cows.

Her owner was riding her out with some other boarders at the stable. They took a route that required them to pass a farm with cows. Xena took one look and came completely unglued. Her owner managed to stay on and get her to stand long enough so she could dismount and hand-walk her closer to the strange beasts that were terrifying her. Eyes wide, heart pounding, and shaking all over, Xena followed her owner toward the fence, but once they got within fifty feet of the closest cow Xena planted her feet and refused to go any closer. She had now also broken into a sweat and was actively trying to back away from these foreign animals. Her owner decided to take her back to the barn and calm her down. She walked her out of eyesight of the cows, remounted, and rode back to the barn. As soon as the cows were out of sight, Xena relaxed and became her usual quiet self.

Confident she could get her mare past this bump in the road, her owner came out again the next day. She just hand-walked her to where the cows were pastured and planned on staying there all day to let Xena hand graze in a patch of grass next to the fence. As soon as they approached the cows, Xena again became frantic, breathing heavy, shaking, and sweating. Her owner called me and I suggested retreating to a point that Xena was comfortable and allowing her to graze and relax. Then slowly get closer to the cows, each time allowing her to graze and relax again. A short while later I got another call saying Xena would not relax as long as she could see the cows. Her owner took Xena back to the barn.

As circumstances had it, her owner was leaving that boarding facility to a different one within the next week, so the cows would be inaccessible for further desensitization. After hearing about Xena's reaction, and knowing how quiet and willing this horse usually is, I had already categorized cows as a phobia for Xena. Given the change in boarding facilities and the unlikelihood that they would come across cows anytime again, we dropped the subject.

Enter the county fair several years later. Xena's owner was allowing a 4-H member to show her at the county fair. As you know, county fairs have cows. Again we were faced with the phobia. Xena would not even eat if she could see the cows. We had to strategically schedule her being out of her stall with the cows being in the vicinity. Seeing her reactions first-hand allowed me to truly categorize Xena's fear of the cows as an actual phobia. Xena's normally completely trusting and confidant personality, coupled with the drastic physical effects (increased respiration, trembling, increased heart rate, sweating, and overall fearful demeanor that did not decrease with repeated or lengthy exposure to the stimulus) was all the evidence I needed. Cows were not going to be in Xena's future.

I have known numerous horses with phobias. While quite uncommon, they do exist and need to be recognized. Xena's owner had people suggest keeping her in a pasture or turnout with a cow to get over it. This works with fears but not phobias. I have seen people try and force the issue with a phobia with disastrous consequences. Horse will run through fences, climb stall walls, run into objects, and overall have a complete disregard for their own well-being and ours. Enlist the help of a trainer if you are not sure whether your horse just has a fear or has an actual phobia.

Excessive spooking, whether due to actual fear or just a desire to play a game, can not only be frustrating, but dangerous and scary too. Identifying why your horse is spooking is the key to developing a proper and effective plan of action to improve the situation.

CHAPTER 9
CATCH ME IF YOU CAN!

"The horse. Here is nobility without conceit, friendship without envy, beauty without vanity. A willing servant, yet never a slave." *~Ronald Duncan*

We've all fallen victim to this less than fun game that horses play – running away when we try to get them from the pasture. For us it can be frustrating, irritating, a complete waste of all our ride time, and more! To our horse, it can range from being simply a fun game, to an unwillingness to leave the herd or pasture, or to being afraid or unsure about the person or the work that will ensue.

The game can vary from the horse simply evading the halter being put on, to kicking out and running full tilt away from the person trying to catch them. The horse's timing and body language can give us clues to the cause. Do they run to the end of the paddock as soon as you open the gate? Do they stand quietly and let you approach and then duck out and walk away as you attempt to put on the halter? Do they let you catch them in the afternoon but not the morning? All of these things, along with consideration of your horse's demeanor (playful, aggressive, fearful, etc.) will give us clues to why they are exhibiting this behavior. Again, as always, we need to figure out the cause of the behavior in order to eradicate it.

Leo's story

I received the text while giving a lesson: "I can't catch Leo!" The student I would be instructing the following hour could not catch her horse. I wish I could say this was the first time this had happened, but it wasn't. I excused myself momentarily from the lesson and walked out to the paddock. Leo was happily cantering circles around his owner who had resorted to angry name calling and throwing the halter at him. In case you were wondering, this is not an effective solution. I opened the gate, picked up the halter and stood quietly. Leo stopped and stared at me for a moment and then approached in a reserved and disappointed manner. I had ruined his game.

Why did Leo come to me but not his owner? Simple, I refused to play his game. It's no fun when we don't become emotional and interact with them. I had worked with Leo plenty of times over the past few years and he would occasionally try to bait me into his wonderful game. I simply refused. Granted, I have the time to ignore him and walk quietly towards him and work him calmly around the arena if he insists on being difficult to catch. Quiet determination is the key to catching the game player.

The first time Leo attempted this game with me it took quite a while, probably around 30 minutes, to convince him it wasn't fun or productive. I would refuse to become emotional or "chase" him. When Leo stopped, I quietly approached him. If he chose to leave and not be caught, I turned his playful antics into work. I pushed him around the paddock, changing his direction and driving him forward until I could tell he wanted to stop. Then I pushed him a little longer, and only then allowed him to take a break. At this point I would approach him quietly again and let him make the decision about being brought in or not. Every time he tried to avoid me, I made him work.

It's important to have a turnout area that is conducive to this exercise. A large pasture or a paddock with lots of horses in it is not as easy to work with. If you can arrange to make the turnout smaller and have only a few other horses to contend with, it is a much easier process.

It didn't take long for Leo to figure this process out. It was no longer his game; I had taken control and refused to play by his rules so he simply gave up. This in turn actually caused him to start to come to me in the paddock. Leo was a smart horse who actually liked attention and doing a job, so when his game was taken away he was more than eager to move on to the day's events.

It wasn't so easy for his owner. Not only had she routinely participated in the game, but she did not seem to have the patience and persistence to execute the needed method to resolve it. It is always harder once the horse has exploited your weakness and now you are trying to convince him you have become a determined and unrelenting force. They keep waiting for you to lose your temper and succumb to mindless swearing and halter throwing. They are convinced that, if they play long enough, this result will occur as it always has in the past. It is going to take more time and patience than it would if you had never made the wrong choice in the first place. Eventually I was able to convince her of this and, when executed persistently, the method worked just as well for her as it did for me. Leo's "catch me if you can" fun was over!

Khan's story

Khan was one of those horses that seemed to truly dislike anything having to do with people. He would tolerate his owner and his job but certainly did not enjoy it. One day he had the revelation that he could avoid people all together if he simply refused to be caught.

After numerous days of being unable to get a halter on her horse, Khan's owner finally approached me for help. I first wanted to see the whole situation, so I asked her to show me a typical workout for Khan. We had the barn owner leave him in for the day and I observed a normal workout between Khan and his owner. I immediately identified the problem.

Khan's owner was very detail orientated and nit-picked every little mistake to the point of total frustration to the horse. She heavily disciplined the slightest of infractions and never encouraged or praised things done well. He was made to do the same maneuver over and over without relief until he had done it absolutely perfectly. His owner was behaving similar to a drill sergeant, and the horse resented it.

Khan didn't want to be caught outside because he simply dreaded the work that he knew was coming. Not only did he have a dislike for people in general, but now he had a valid reason for disliking them! He couldn't win; his efforts were never good enough in his owner's eyes. This was the problem to be addressed, not the catching in the paddock.

We started with lessons twice a week where I taught his owner to encourage and praise, to make his work less repetitive and add new and interesting things to his repertoire. We added trail obstacles on a daily basis, one day the bridge, the next day the gate, etc. Khan's owner was only allowed to work on an exercise for a certain amount of time then she had to change topics. I taught her to recognize the horse trying, and to look for progress not perfection.

We had the horse left inside in the mornings for several weeks while we worked on the real issue at hand. Khan would be turned out after his work was completed and he was free to enjoy his day. After reformatting Khan's workouts he became less crabby and standoffish and became more willing and cooperative. Seeing this change, we started turning him out in the morning and bringing him in to work about an hour before evening feeding time. After he was worked and properly cooled out, he got to go to his stall and eat.

The concept was to get Khan to be more willing to work by modifying how his owner handled him during their workouts, and then giving him additional positive reinforcement afterwards. For the first several weeks, that meant getting to go out and play/socialize for the rest of the day. For the next stretch of time, he was able to go to his stall and eat after his workouts.

Now the moment of truth: going to get Khan in the middle of the day. What happened? He let his owner approach him and slip his halter on and he willingly followed her to the barn. Success!

In Khan's case, he had chosen to resist being caught because he was frustrated and discouraged with his work program. Add that to the fact that he already had a dislike for anything related to people, and it was a recipe for disaster. By allowing him to be more successful in his workouts and eliminating the rigorous and mind-numbing repetition of exercises, while adding in a positive end to his sessions, we were able to eliminate the behavior.

Imagine going to work or school every day knowing you were going to get nothing but criticism and would have to repeat every task or exercise until you did it absolutely perfectly. In these cases, if you were given the option to not show up, wouldn't you take it? Of course you would! In a job like that you would most definitely quit if it were an option. With school you would complain to your parents and your counselor and try to get things changed. Khan's solution was to avoid being brought in altogether.

CHAPTER 10
SOUR HORSES

"Riding a horse is not a gentle hobby, to be picked up and laid down like a game of solitaire. It is a grand passion, it seizes person whole and once it has done so, one will have to accept that one's life will be radically changed."   *~Ralph Waldo Emerson*

When we refer to "sourness" in horses it can have a wide range of meanings. It usually means that a horse exhibits negative behaviors consistently when they are put in certain specific situations. The three most common "sourness" occurrences are barn sour, buddy sour, and ring sour. Another related and common affliction is a horse becoming ring wise.

A barn sour horse is one that gets upset, exhibits negative behaviors, and becomes difficult to work with when they are away from their "home." This can refer to trail horses that don't like to ride away from the property to show horses who don't like to load in the trailer to leave the property.

Buddy sour horses exhibit these negative behaviors when

asked to leave another horse or even another animal such as a goat, dog, sheep, etc. The barn sour or buddy sour horse may get upset when the "home" or "friend" is a mere 10 feet away and you are walking away from it, or when they can no longer see, hear, or smell it. Some horses are fine for short periods of time but fall apart the longer they are away from home or their friend. Each horse has a different threshold for withdrawal but it always interferes with their work and usually escalates over time if not addressed.

Behaviors range from refusing to leave the property or other animal altogether by planting their feet and refusing to move, repeated calling out as you're attempting to leave, repeatedly trying to turn around, attempting to run back to the barn or friend, rearing and/or bucking when they are not allowed to go back, agitated "jigging" or head shaking, chewing on the bit, moving sideways and backing up and more.

Ring sour horses exhibit negative behaviors when entering the show environment or within the show/class itself. These horses exhibit negative behavior usually due to some unpleasantness or negative emotion associated with the show pen/environment. Ring sour horses exhibit behaviors at a show such as refusing to enter the ring, exhibiting negative behaviors within a class that are out of character for that horse, getting agitated, nervous, upset when asked to line up at the cones for a pattern, etc. Any horse exhibiting consistent negative behavior that is triggered by the show atmosphere or situation can be classified as "ring sour."

Ring wise horses engage in certain behaviors because they have become "wise" to the show pen protocol. They listen to the announcer and/or anticipate transitions or certain maneuvers, behave poorly, or perform sloppily in the show pen. This usually happens after they discover the unwillingness of their rider to reprimand or correct them within an actual class, due to the possibility of getting marked down or not placing. They have learned that they can "get away" with certain things within a class that they normally cannot in a schooling/work session. This can escalate to downright dangerous behavioral problems that we discussed earlier in the book. These behaviors stem from the horse's belief that they can do whatever they want within a class without having to worry about the usual consequences for their behavior.

Red's story

Red was a handsome bay gelding that was meant to be his owner's trail horse. Red and his owner had been on several trail rides that had gone well, and it seemed to be a good match with a promising future.

One afternoon Red's owner came out shortly before feeding time to take a short ride around the property. He normally came out midafternoon to ride, but he had a project he was working on at the office and would need to stay at work later for the next few weeks. He saddled up Red and started off around the fields. Halfway across the first field, Red stopped and tried to turn around to head back to the barn. His owner turned him back around and several minutes later asked Red to trot. Again Red stopped and tried to turn around. This time he pinned his ears and refused to head back away from the barn. After several minutes of fruitless efforts to get him to trot away from the barn, Red's owner gave up and headed back, thinking Red was just hungry and wanted his evening feeding.

Returning the next day after work, Red's owner brought him in and let him eat a portion of his hay before he saddled up, confidant that if Red wasn't hungry he would be more willing to ride away from the barn during feeding time. He was wrong. Halfway across the first field Red stopped and refused to go any further again. Knowing he couldn't be that hungry his owner became more insistent and aggressive in his cues to turn away from the barn and trot off as he had asked. At this point Red started swishing his tail and tossing his head as he spun around in circles trying to go back to the barn while his rider insisted they continue riding away from the barn. Frustrated, Red's owner stopped to rest for a moment. At this point Red took the opportunity to try and head back to the barn at a little quicker pace. He picked up a strong trot and when his owner picked up to slow him and turn him back around he gave a little buck. Startled and intimidated, as Red had never acted like that before, his owner again asked him to stop and Red finally listened. Slightly shaken up he promptly got off of Red and walked back to the barn.

The next day Red's owner left work early and decided to try taking him out one more time on his own when it wasn't feeding time. He was hoping that Red would behave better if he took him out well before evening feeding time. Just in case it didn't go smoothly, he had taken time to bolster his confidence and made the decision that he was going to make Red listen this time. He swung into the saddle and headed away from the barn. This time they didn't even make it halfway across the field before the disagreement began.

Taking a deep breath and gritting his teeth, Red's owner gave him a good heel kick and a spanking across the hindquarters to get him to continue across the field on the trail ride he intended to take. Red again gave a little buck and threw his head. This time his owner continued his more aggressive approach and Red hit the brakes and hopped up in the front end a bit. Intimidated, his rider backed off for a moment to get his nerve back up. He spanked him and gave him another heel kick and this time Red hopped up a little higher in the front. Frustrated he began yanking on the reins and pulling Red around in circles, at which time Red started trotting sideways back to the barn. Pulling on the reins harder to try and regain some control, his owner desperately tried to stop Red. When Red finally stopped a few yards from the barn doors, his rider tried again to turn him away and head back to the field. Red planted his feet and again started hopping up in the front end.

Having had enough, and now getting quite nervous, his owner dismounted and took him into the indoor arena to work him.

Surprisingly, Red worked very nicely in the indoor and displayed none of the negative behaviors that he had outside. His owner took him back outside and attempted to ride away from the barn again. Red again refused, throwing his head and jigging sideways back toward the barn doors. Frustrated and tired, the man gave up and put Red away, already pulling out his phone to call some friends and get some advice. The advice was overwhelmingly in favor of finding a trainer. He found me.

After hearing the whole story from Red's owner, I knew we were dealing with a simple case of Red being barn sour. I came out and first rode Red for a few days in the indoor and outdoor arenas to get a feel for the horse. It would do no good to jump on and try to ride him out away from the barn before I had established a relationship with Red. With a horse that has exhibited behaviors like Red's, it is important to make sure it has a good concept of yielding his head and hindquarter in a controlled environment. I checked these things out, made sure he had a good foundation and, after getting a solid idea of Red's personality and level of training, which was quite good, we were ready to head out away from the barn.

With a horse such as Red that has exhibited somewhat assertive negative behavior, I do not simply point his head in a direction and go. The ideal situation is to be actively asking the sour horse to do a job and keep their mind off of the fact we are leaving the sanctity of the barn. Undoubtedly the horse will realize we are heading away from the barn, but I now have a more solid reason and venue for correcting any negative behaviors. As we talked about in the chapter on extreme spooking, we do not focus on or discipline the act as much as we discipline the decision to not do the job we are asking of the horse.

With Red, I started by asking him to do shallow serpentines and incorporated bend as we made our way away from the barn. This way, if he leaned back toward the barn or started to refuse to continue away from the barn, I could redirect him into the bending and serpentine work instead of just trying to keep pointing him away from the barn. Since Red had progressed past mild objections into actively insisting on not leaving the barn area with his owner, I of course expected him to have some "tantrums" with me even with the work redirection.

Several times Red tried to stop and turn, I yielded his head, disengaged his hindquarters, using the end of the rein to reinforce my leg if he refused to move his feet. Once I accomplished this I put him right back into the exercises we had been working on before his objection occurred. Several times Red escalated into half rears, head shaking, and moving sideways in the direction of the barn. At these times, I got after his hindquarters more aggressively with my leg and the end of the rein to get him refocused on yielding his hip and back on track with the exercises we were doing. The intensity of the request and cues for the requests increased as his negative behavior decisions increased in intensity. After about a half hour, Red gave up his attempts at trying to get back to the barn and focused on me and what I was asking of him. We walked, trotted and cantered in serpentine fashion while heading away from and eventually back to the barn.

On our way back toward the barn, Red gave me another expected maneuver as he became focused on getting back quickly. Each time Red made the decision to try and get back to the barn on his own, we headed back away from the barn, incorporating bending exercises and transitions until he refocused on me. Believe it or not, if you use this technique your horse will actually start to slow down on their own when they realize they are heading back home, to avoid further work!

When we got back to the barn I did not simply put Red away. We worked around the barn and in the indoor arena for a good twenty minutes before he was untacked and put away. Using this method for several weeks, Red got to the point where he would ride away from the barn willingly without having to be constantly mentally occupied with exercises and maneuvers to keep him behaving well. With strict instructions to put him to work quickly if the behavior seemed to start to recur, I left Red and his owner to enjoy their trail riding days.

It is extremely common for horses to become barn sour. The habit occurs anytime the horse decides home is better and easier than your intended outing for the day. To discourage this behavior, take your horse out at all different times of the day to discourage reluctance to go out during certain times, including feeding times. Always return to the barn slower than you left. I make my horses walk quietly whenever we are headed back to the barn. I never trot, canter, or even allow them to walk faster when we are on our way back. If they attempt to increase the speed, put them to work heading away from the barn again.

Avoid immediately untacking and putting your horse away when you return. Work them either around the barn or in the arena(s) so they avoid the common "when I get home I'm done" outlook. Make the ride away from the barn as fun and relaxing as you can. Keep your horse listening to you and check in with them frequently so they don't forget about you, but don't be a crabby drill sergeant if they are going along quietly and willingly. Putting them to work, giving them a job to do and something to focus on at the first sign of a problem is always a good idea. Implementing these guidelines will help prevent your horse from becoming barn sour, and keep a previously sour horse from relapsing.

Brandi's story

Brandi was a pretty little bay mare that was a dream in the show pen and on the trail. Her owner was an experienced teenage girl who loved to socialize while riding. One spring a new boarder arrived, and the new girl and Brandi's owner quickly hit it off and became inseparable. They arranged their riding times so they could ride together most days and had fun planning their summer show and trail riding schedules for the year. After several months of riding together almost daily, the girls had their first show of the season. They trailered together, got their horses ready together, and were excited for their classes as both horses had been riding wonderfully.

The first few classes they had together couldn't have gone better! They kept swapping back and forth from first and second place. One class Brandi's owner would win and the new girl would get second, the next class Brandi's owner would get second and the new girl would win. How perfect, right!?

Then disaster struck. The new girl didn't enjoy competing in the pattern classes of equitation and horsemanship, so she put her horse away and came back out to watch Brandi and her rider show; they loved pattern classes and always did quite well.

In the short amount of time it took her to put her horse back in the barn and return to the show pen, Brandi had worked up into a frenzy. She was whinnying and spinning circles and had broken into a sweat. Confused, Brandi's owner did her best to get her refocused and practice her pattern in the warm up pen, but it was useless, Brandi was mentally checked out. The new girl went back to the barn to get a lunge line and noticed her horse was also acting strangely. She was pacing her stall and whinnying, ignoring the hay she had been given before her owner left to watch Brandi. By the time the new girl retrieved the lunge line, Brandi's owner was bringing her back to the barn in tears. The show steward had asked her to leave the warm up pen, as Brandi's spinning and antics were dangerous to the other horses and competitors.

Frustrated, she began untacking Brandi and noticed that she had now settled down and was standing quietly. Her friend's horse had also quieted down and was eating her hay. After putting Brandi away and regaining her composure, her owner had calmed down enough to eat some lunch. She would tack up Brandi for the afternoon pleasure classes, and was hoping for better behavior. It would be more fun anyway, as her new friend would be competing in pleasure also.

Tacked up and ready to go, the girls headed to the warm up pen and had a phenomenal afternoon, placing first and second in all four classes! Convinced Brandi's behavior had been a fluke, they went home happy and content with the day.

The following day Brandi's owner went out to the barn by herself, as her friend wasn't feeling well and decided to stay home and rest. She tacked up Brandi and headed out for a trail ride. After only about five minutes, Brandi started acting strangely. She started to whinny and become agitated, prancing nervously and throwing her head. Concerned, her owner dismounted and checked all the tack. Nothing seemed amiss so she remounted and tried to continue. Again Brandi started with the unusual behavior. Now more concerned, her owner headed back to the barn to talk to the stable owner and ask her to check Brandi over and see if something was wrong. When she returned to the barn, her friend's horse was pacing the fence line and also acting upset. She put Brandi in her stall and went up to the house to ask the stable owner for her opinion on the situation.

After explaining the behavior to the stable owner, she was a little insulted when the stable owner started to laugh a bit. She explained to Brandi's owner that her horse and her friend's horse weren't sick or hurt or anything of the sort, they were buddy sour! She gave her my name and number and told her to give me a call.

I drove out to meet Brandi's owner, her friend and the two horses. I explained to them that while they had become great friends and riding buddies, so had their horses. We needed to separate the two and get them acclimated to being ridden without the other again. They would need to refocus their horses on their jobs and riders and off of each other. Unfortunately, that also meant the girls had to ride separately and without each other. The first few rides were going to be the roughest, so we set them up as formal lessons, at separate times, for both girls, so I could help with the process.

Brandi's owner's lesson was extremely difficult, as Brandi was dead set on not paying attention to her rider and only on where her equine buddy was. After lots of different steering and transition drills she finally settled down for a short period and we wrapped up while she was quiet. The friend's lesson was much easier. Her horse was only mildly agitated and settled in quickly once we were able to refocus her on her work.

Several weeks went by and Brandi was still giving her owner trouble riding without her friend. It took her extremely long periods of time to settle down and she would only settle down for short periods at a time. It was time for the next step. I suggested to Brandi's owner that we move Brandi to another barn for a period of time so she could reconnect with her owner and emotionally detach from the other horse. When the horse cannot see, smell, or hear the other horse, the process becomes easier. When the horse is being stalled next to and/or turned out with the horse they have become attached to, the process can be harder and take longer.

We moved Brandi to a small boarding facility about five miles away. Usually the horse has a rough short term adjustment period where they may be distressed, stop eating for a while and so on, but it is usually short-lived, as the other horse is completely out of the picture. This was the case with Brandi. It took her three days to calm down and begin to act and eat more normally. At this point, her owner started regular lessons and we worked on building the relationship back up between horse and rider.

After six weeks and a lot of hard work, Brandi was ready to go back to her regular boarding stable. We made arrangements to have her stalled as far away from her old friend as possible, and to be turned out in separate paddocks. Arrangements were made initially between Brandi's owner and her friend so that for the first few weeks they wouldn't ride together at all. After that they could ride at the same time, but they needed to stay focused on working their horses and not walking side by side or standing around talking. They were not to enter or leave the arena together. For the rest of the summer they needed to trailer to shows separately and stall their horses away from each other. These tactics worked well and both girls were able to enjoy the rest of the summer with their horses, trail riding and showing, keeping the new restrictions in mind.

Buddy sour horses can range from being mildly distracted and agitated when separated from their friend to becoming all out uncontrollable. They might only mind being apart when they can't hear or smell each other, or they might get upset when the other is out of sight at all. Being aware of horses' tendencies to become attached to each other, it is important to remember that when you're riding you have a job to do. You need to stay focused on your horse and keep your horse focused on you. That's not to say you can't talk and relax and have fun during your rides, but you need to be aware of how much time you spend doing it. Certain horses also show a predisposition to becoming attached to others, while others are more independent. You will need to recognize which type your horse is, and ride accordingly.

Buddy sourness in horses can develop over years or simply take a few weeks/months. In general, the longer a horse has been with and not separated from another, the more attached they get and the harder it is to get past. But, it can be done with time, patience, determination, and sometimes a physical separation for a period of time. Establishing and maintaining a strong working relationship between yourself and your horse can also help curb attachment tendencies.

Maverick's story

Grand champion hunter under saddle, grand champion huntseat equitation, grand champion junior showmanship, and the list goes on. Maverick was an exceptional show horse, a beautiful mover with a great show ring presence. For years his young rider took him to every show within 500 miles of home. Every weekend they were gone, cleaning up wherever they went.

One spring, while prepping for the first show of the season, Maverick started becoming agitated at the start cone for the patterns his rider had him practicing. They had started to practice more involved and complicated patterns, as she would be moving up an age group this year and the patterns would be more difficult.

It started with the occasional sidestep, then slowly progressed to backing up and head tossing. The more they practiced, the more upset Maverick got. Abandoning patterns for a while they focused on pleasure, and Maverick reverted back to the quiet, willing horse he had always been. At the first show he cleaned up in pleasure, but equitation was another story. As he approached the start cone, we could see his body tense up. As his owner asked him to stand and wait to be acknowledged, he started dancing in place. Just as the judge looked over to acknowledge them, Maverick started backing up toward the gate and refused to go up to the start cone. They were excused and asked to leave the ring. Once back in the warm up pen, his owner ran him through the elements of the pattern and he did beautifully. Convinced he was over whatever had been bothering him and that she had her sweet, cooperative boy back, she prepared for their next equitation class.

As they approached the start cone, his rider tensed up. Nervous about the difficult pattern and the disaster in the previous class, she became anxious. Maverick tensed up and planted his feet, refusing to go any farther. His owner, now angry, got after him quite aggressively, at which point he started to hop up in front and execute some half rears. They were excused again. Now terribly frustrated, she started to ride him extremely aggressively in the warm up pen. Kicking and pulling, she rode him hard until he was sweaty and breathing hard. Satisfied she had taught him a lesson, she cooled him out and untacked him. They had day two of the show tomorrow and she was confidant his patterns would be perfect.

The next day Maverick was in a sour mood from the start. Usually a happy horse, he was pinning his ears and swishing his tail in the warm-up ring. Frustrated, his owner turned up the pressure working him harder and demanding more with every passing minute. When it was time to enter the ring for their first pleasure class, Maverick refused to go through the gate. He planted his feet and then backed away from the entry gate. One of the show attendants led him into the pen and released his bridle as he went through the gate. Maverick made one lap around and, when he passed the entry gate again, he stopped and stepped sideways towards it. When his owner tried to turn him away and get him going again he threw his head and refused. They were excused again. The rest of the day went downhill from there. Most classes Maverick refused to enter, and the ones his owner got him into he only made it around one lap before being excused for unruly behavior.

Arriving back to the stable in tears that night, Maverick's owner told her mom she was done showing and stormed out to the car. Her mom put Maverick away and they drove home. After a few days to cool off, Maverick's owner came back out to the barn determined to make Maverick listen. She started by having a fairly good ride but kept pushing him to do everything absolutely perfectly, and finally Maverick blew up. He pinned his ears and gave a few half rears and a few small bucks, and attempted to leave the arena and go back in the barn with his owner still hanging on. This time I happened to be in the arena giving a lesson and saw the whole thing. I had heard about the problems, but they were not my clients so I hadn't asked or pushed the issue.

After seeing this display I called Maverick's owner's mom and had a brief talk with her about my thoughts on the situation. I was concerned for her daughter's safety and for Maverick's sanity. She agreed to set up a lesson for her daughter the next day. I made the stipulation that she had to be present for her daughter's entire lesson because I needed to explain some things to them about what was going on.

I began by riding Maverick myself to see if my hunches were right. I put him through his paces and slowly increased my demands on him. Acknowledging his efforts and appreciating when he was trying to please me, we had a beautiful ride. I then had his owner ride. She immediately started picking on him for every little thing with no reward when things were done correctly and a harsh reprimand for the slightest infractions. It didn't take long for Maverick to blow up. It was time to talk.

I had heard the story from the beginning the night before from the mother. It had all started with the increased pressure of moving up an age group and working on harder patterns. Maverick's owner had pushed him too hard too fast and didn't acknowledge when he was trying to please her at all. He must have felt he had no way of getting a reprieve, so he became distressed and defensive. What started as patterns trickled over into all of his work as his owner became more frustrated and displeased with him. He had gone from being her pride and joy, getting constant praise for a job well done, to being a disappointment and getting nothing but negativity from his rider.

This all came to a head at the last show when he saw that start cone and felt his rider become tense and anxious because he had been struggling with the harder patterns at home. When practicing in the warm up pen after that first problematic class, without cones, and with less pressure, Maverick had managed to pull it together. Upon reentering the show pen and again being confronted with the cones and an angry rider, he again objected to the situation. The problem was exacerbated by being excused and allowed to leave after refusing to do the pattern.

Maverick soon shut down on his rider completely when she became more and more demanding in the warm up pen, a place where she had usually always been more relaxed and easygoing, versus the show pen where she was, as exhibitors usually are, more tense. He was now refusing to do even the pleasure class due to the high amount of emotion and stress involved. Even at home, he was upset as he could pick up on his rider's level of aggression and displeasure towards him.

We needed to start over. His owner needed to step back and again see Maverick for the amazing animal he was. Once we could get back on track I would be able to help her progress him to being competitive in the harder age divisions, but for now we needed to rebuild the bond between horse and rider.

We began by having Maverick's owner ask him to perform very simple tasks, things he had been doing successfully for several years. I forced his rider to smile throughout the ride and praise him excessively for every accomplishment. Eventually she slid back into her old mind frame of loving her gelding, and was smiling and praising him on her own. When we reintroduced patterns, we started without cones and very simply. When we reintroduced the cones we simply rode around them, not using them as markers for maneuvers. Over the next week we started lining up at a start cone and then just calmly walking down the center of the arena. We progressed slowly until Maverick was back at his previous level of performance within pleasure and patterns.

It was time to go to a show. We picked a small show nearby to work on his ring sourness. I was fully aware that he would most likely behave similarly to his last show, remembering the negative experiences from his rider and the reinforcement of getting to leave the pen when he acted up.

I approached the ring steward before the show started and explained to him we had a ring sour horse and could he please not excuse him and let his rider finish the class if he acted up? Having done this before, I was confidant the judge would be agreeable and she was. If you've been showing long enough, you will come across a ring sour horse that needs some work and you become very understanding to others in that situation.

We warmed up casually and without much demand on Maverick. When it was time to enter the first pleasure class, Maverick was tense but he went in. I had his owner talk to him quietly and in an encouraging manner. Here was the next important step – I had them walk the entire class. No transitions, no pressure, just walking. I needed Maverick to become comfortable in the show pen again. As the class progressed I could see him go from tense and resistant, to confused, then to relax. The next class they walked and trotted, but didn't emphasize collection or extension of stride too much. By the third class Maverick was entering without hesitation and went past the entry gates without hesitation.

By the last pleasure class, Maverick was able to ride the actual class completely and actually won. It was time to go home. The next weekend there was another small local show that I took them to. This time we would enter a few equitation classes also. They had worked all week on simple patterns with little to no emphasis put on the cones. Pleasure classes went smoothly, he won them all. Next, equitation; we ran through the pattern in the warm up pen and it went well. Maverick entered the show pen and eyed up the cones. I had his rider start the pattern several feet away from the cone and execute the required transitions and maneuvers either before or after the cones, not at them. Maverick completed the pattern successfully. Of course they didn't place, but we were on the right track.

We attended two more, smaller shows and proceeded this way until Maverick was behaving perfectly in both pleasure and pattern classes. No hint of nervousness or agitation. At home we had been slowly progressing his work to prepare him for his next regular show where the competition would be harder. Acknowledging his efforts and taking her time with Maverick, his owner was able to successfully take him to the next level. Time for the next step, returning to the circuit they had been competing on. I kept his rider distracted and relaxed and the show went perfectly. They placed well but, more importantly, Maverick stayed calm and collected the entire time.

Ring sourness can occur for many different reasons. In Maverick's case the pressure of being more competitive caused his owner to become a more aggressive and picky rider, focused on perfection not progress. This mentality is highly detrimental to the horse. They feel as if they can't win and they either shut down or blow up. When this is exacerbated in the show pen, due to even higher demands and expectations, the negative behaviors come out in the classes. At most shows, the horse and rider are excused to prevent interference with other exhibitor's rides and to keep everyone safe and the show moving along. This compounds the problem by letting the horse leave the arena after exhibiting the behavior we don't want. The method we used with Maverick is highly successful in these cases.

Other reasons for being ring sour can be that a horse is simply nervous in the show environment. Being around a lot of strange horses and in new environments can be upsetting to the horse and negative behaviors arise. Gradually desensitizing your horse to other horses and new environments can work well in this case. Go to smaller shows in less intimidating environments frequently and allow your horse to adjust. Work on confidence and trust-building exercises with the horse that will carry over into the show environment.

Doing too many classes without adequate rest or food and water can cause a horse to become sour and resistant to showing. Allowing breaks for eating, drinking and unwinding is highly important. Make the show pen pleasant and comfortable for your horse. Make showing a fun rewarding experience, not a stressful, unsettling one.

Ring wise horses become tuned in to the normal routine in the show pen and start to anticipate transitions and maneuvers, causing you to do poorly in the class. Changing things up and just walking a class or a pattern can be useful. Not performing transitions or maneuvers exactly when they are asked for can help also.

Horses sometimes stumble onto bad behaviors and discover the miracle of being excused. A poorly-fitting show saddle that pinches can cause a horse to buck in the show pen, getting them excused. If this happens several times before the cause is discovered then, voila, you have a ring sour turned ring wise horse.

Overall, sour horses are horses that have a negative or insecure outlook on being away from their home, their pasture mates, or within a show atmosphere. As with all other behavioral issues, it is important to understand why your horse may be developing these behaviors and deal with them accordingly. Establishing and maintaining a relationship where your horse looks to you for confidence and guidance when they are feeling upset or insecure will go a long way in preventing, limiting, and recovering from being sour. If you become and continue to be the most important thing in your horse's life while you are together, most of these situations will not occur in the first place. When we lose that relationship, or fail to gain it in the first place, it opens the doors for negative behaviors to pop up.

CHAPTER 11
ODDS AND ENDS

"A horse can lend its rider the speed and strength he or she lacks - but the rider who is wise remembers it is no more than a loan." ~Pam Brown

There are numerous other behavioral issues that can occur with your horse. In this chapter I will discuss some of them and their causes on a smaller scale. Read on for insight into trailering issues, aggression issues, pulling while tied, cinchiness (exhibiting negative behaviors when saddled) and more.

Trailering

Let's begin this section by again looking at the situation from your horse's perspective. We ask them to enter a relatively small box. Add to that the fact that horses have different depth perception and visual fields than we do, and the trailer can sometimes look like a gaping black cavern to your horse. Then we ask them to stand quietly while we drive at various speeds, hitting potholes and dealing with ignorant people who cut us off and force us to maneuver our rig in unexpected and unpleasant ways. Let's be honest, I know we all do it: at times when we have to execute a maneuver while hauling that we know is going to be unsettling to our horse, we apologize to our cargo as if they can hear us, for putting them through certain evasive driving maneuvers. We then unload our horse somewhere strange and new, which is usually accompanied by something involving work or other unpleasantness. Whether it's a long trail ride, a horse show, or a trailer-in visit to the vet, when we unload our horse they know they aren't simply going to be able to relax the day away. Given these circumstances, it's amazing we get horses to load, travel, and unload as easily as we do!

Most horses will at one point or another have a small problem with some aspect of trailering, whether it's refusing to load, behaving poorly inside the trailer or unloading in a less than graceful or anticipated manner. These things do happen, and the occasional misbehavior in trailering is not uncommon. The problem occurs when the horse consistently refuses to load, acts up after loading during the ride or in the trailer before unloading, or consistently unloads in an unpleasant manner that can escalate to flying backwards or leaping off the trailer.

Horses that experience anxiety when faced with trailering have usually had a bad experience, or have never been worked with enough to understand the situation or trust their handler. Horses that are calm about trailering situations but simply flat out refuse can be exhibiting resistance and dominance issues that may be a direct reflection of areas of handling and training that are not solid enough to carry over when asking the animal to participate in an activity that can be quite unsettling, scary, and unpleasant in the horses eyes. Another variation is buddy, barn, or show sour horses that avoid trailering in an effort to not leave home or their friends, or go to a show.

Lastly, ignorance on behalf of the handler can influence a horse's behavior when loading, hauling, and unloading. I've seen people stand directly in front of their horse, facing the horse, and ask them to load into the trailer. Do you really want your horse to jump on top of you? Reckless driving on behalf of the hauler can also cause a horse anxiety about trailering. Remember that you have precious cargo back there, drive accordingly! There are endless arrays of hauler error that can make a horse decide trailering is not something they wish to do.

Foundation

When training a horse to trailer well, the loading, hauling, and unloading process can reflect how well you have instilled groundwork manners overall. If there are any holes or weaknesses in your horse's groundwork or your handling, they have a tendency to rear their ugly head during trailering. If your horse does not willingly follow you without resistance, does not yield well to pressure, does not back well, does not stand tied quietly, and so on, it can make loading, hauling, and unloading your horse difficult.

Physical discomfort

If you have gone back over your groundwork and solidified all the necessary aspects of it, we can look to other causes and solutions. The first thing we can look for is a physical cause. In this case we look at the horse's comfort getting into, out of, and standing in the trailer. For instance, a horse with arthritic knees might resist a big step up or step down and may do better with a ramp load trailer. An exceptionally tall, wide, or long horse may be cramped standing in a smaller trailer and may need one with more room. Your trailer might not have proper ventilation on warm days and the horse becomes hot and uncomfortable in the trailer. These are some of the numerous physical comfort-based reasons a horse may object to trailering.

Fear

If a horse seems highly agitated or nervous about trailering, they may not have had a good foundation in learning to load, haul, and /or unload. It's also possible the horse had a trailering accident or bad experience that has caused the anxiety about trailering. Going back and getting the horse relaxed about the situation will go a long way. Practice loading, standing, and unloading, religiously and with positive rewards for the horse. Let them just stand and relax and eat some hay in the trailer, feed them their meals in the trailer. Verbal praise and encouragement can also help soothe a nervous horse. You may also want to have a horse along that is extremely experienced and calm about trailering, to assist in calming the anxious horse. The very last thing you want to do is become aggressive with or force a truly nervous horse into the trailering situation. The horse will panic and can severely injure themselves, you, bystanders, and the trailer, and may become even more traumatized about trailering.

Behavioral

Some horses simply decide they would prefer not to be a part of the trailering scenario and will refuse, resist, and/or actively avoid the situation. These horses are not nervous, they respond to their groundwork quite well, have not had a negative experience or any other reason to refuse other than they simply don't want to get in, stand, or get out. In these cases, making the trailer more appealing than the resistance is key. Making their life uncomfortable when they refuse loading by repeatedly and consistently tapping them on the hindquarters with a long whip can be enough to encourage a horse to load. Stop the tapping when they go forward and start again if they plant their feet and refuse, increasing the intensity of the tapping until they go forward again.

If your horse "actively" refuses to load instead of just planting its feet, then making them work is a good place to start. For instance, if your horse avoids the trailer by moving its feet in other ways than forward onto the trailer, then initiating a small lunge circle behind the trailer is beneficial. After you make them move their feet on your terms until they show evidence of wanting to stop and rest, attempt to load again. Every time the horse tries to evade getting in by moving their feet away from the trailer, the intensity of the work increases until the horse decides to load. This technique also works quite well. Your horse will begin to view the trailer as a refuge and place of rest and begin to want to load.

Horses sometimes decide they would rather not stand quietly in the trailer, and exhibit such behaviors as pawing and kicking while in the trailer. Some horses exhibit this behavior due to anxiety, while others use it as their way of demanding to be let out. A good approach is to ignore the horse and leave it in the trailer until it stops the negative behaviors. Only then, unload your horse. Repeat this exercise on days when you have a lot of time to devote and the weather and conditions are conducive. This is a good deterrent for the impatient horse. It will begin to understand that it gets unloaded when it stands quietly and stays in the trailer longer when it acts impatiently.

Unloading

Bolting backward out of the trailer can be a nasty and dangerous habit. Some horses also go the opposite extreme and refuse to unload at all. I approach this behavior differently, depending on whether the bolting out or refusal to unload seems like anticipation to unload, anxiety about the unloading process, or simply a lack of understanding of how to unload properly.

The horse that has anxiety about unloading, or is simply awkward about it, just needs practice and repetition doing it quietly, consistently, and correctly. Making the trailer and trailering experience pleasant for these horses goes a long way. Make frequent short trips that do not end in arriving at a show, the vet clinic, or any other event or place that your horse might find stressful. Going for a short ride and then returning home to a stall with hay or to their pasture with friends can help ease a horse's anxiety. Increasing your horse's overall comfort level with the trailer and hauling can help immensely, but if the behavior continues this is one negative behavior that is best handled by a professional, as it can easily result in injury to you or your horse.

The horse that is simply in a hurry to leave the trailer can be reprimanded for not backing as asked by the handler. The horse that is in a hurry and ignoring its handler when asked to unload nicely needs some more serious work. I reinforce groundwork on backing, making sure to have complete control over the speed and direction of the backing. I then start unloading by asking the horse to back one step and then stepping forward again into the trailer. Quite simply, I work on backing within the confines of the trailer. (As a side note, these exercises are best done initially in a larger, more movement-friendly trailer. Being in the confines of a small trailer can make the environment a lot more dangerous if your horse decides to have a tantrum.) If the horse ignores my cues to back quietly and softly, and flies backwards instead, he is reprimanded and loaded quickly back onto the trailer. Do not allow your horse any down-time or any time away from the trailer if it has bolted out; reload it as soon as possible. Offer a reward when it has unloaded quietly. As I stated previously, this problem can be tricky and dangerous and is best handled by a trainer.

For the horse that refuses to unload, we begin by addressing the issue outside of the trailer and making sure the horse understands back up cues. I use either a short crop or the end of the lead rope on the horse's chest/shoulder to encourage movement, being careful to watch out for the front feet if the horse should attempt to rear or strike out. At this point we are ready to tackle the issue back in the trailer. Ask the horse to back and reinforce with a tap across the chest, as usual increasing the intensity until the horse takes a step backwards. At that point pause, praise, and then continue the process.

Trailering is a science. Most individuals tend to feel overwhelmed and nervous about this daunting task. This is normal. You are putting your beloved animal in a box on wheels, transporting them among other less than courteous drivers on sometimes less than ideal road conditions, and asking them to exit this rolling box in a new environment. Once you become more experienced at loading, hauling, and unloading your horse, you will feel much more relaxed about the situation. Don't be afraid to ask for assistance if you're nervous; your horse will pick up on your anxiety and it will actually cause more problems for you and your horse. It is better to have an experienced friend or trainer assist, until you become confidant, than to try and tackle it all yourself.

The aggressive horse

On occasion, we come across a horse that exhibits aggression for various reasons other than those we covered in previous chapters. These behaviors can vary from simply pinning their ears to flat out attacking a person or other animal. Horses can be food aggressive, stall aggressive, socially aggressive, defensive, aggressive due to physical discomfort or pain, and so on.

Pain or illness

When a typically quiet horse starts demonstrating aggressive behavior, there is always a trigger, you need to find that trigger. As we stated earlier, look for a physical reason first. It is typical for horses to act aggressively when they are not feeling well. Check for injuries, check for oral pain. Is the horse eating, drinking, moving normally, and interacting with other horses as usual? Do they have a fever; do they seem lethargic and dull? Horses with mouth problems, ulcers, fevers, painful injuries, etc. may exhibit signs of aggression. Address these issues first before moving on.

Lack of proper food, water, or exercise

A common source of aggression is not having enough food,

water, or turnout/exercise. If your horse is hungry, thirsty, or has a lot of pent up energy, it may exhibit signs of aggression. An underfed horse may become food aggressive. It will exhibit more severe signs of aggression during feeding times or when asked to leave its food. Expression of the aggression may include ear pinning, charging, attempting to bite or kick, or any combination of these.

A horse that has been left in a stall or small turnout may become aggressive due to pent up energy. I have seen this more times than I can count. You have a well behaved horse that is normally worked or turned out regularly and, due to injury, bad weather, etc., is unable to be worked or turned out, and they become "monsters." I have had clients call me in tears after their normally sweet horse tried to bite, kick, strike, or charge them. The culprit is pent up energy. The horse becomes frustrated and hyper due to lack of exercise, and it comes out in less than acceptable ways. This brings up another of the catch phrases that my clients have come to know and love: It is understandable but not acceptable. While there may be a valid reason for the horse's behavior, we cannot allow the aggressive behavior to continue. The behavior must be disciplined appropriately. Horses sometimes need to be confined due to injury, illness, bad weather and so on that we simply cannot do anything about. If you can, rectify the situation and turn out or exercise your horse regularly. If you cannot, then behavior modification discussed earlier in the book, and in some cases supplements or drugs to lightly sedate your horse, may be in order.

Unrest in the herd

Sometimes horses can become aggressive due to a change in their normal turnout herd. If they are suddenly put with a horse that they do not get along with, they may become aggressive. All horses have small disagreements with each other, but if you suddenly have a horse that is inflicting serious physical or emotional trauma on another you need to assess the situation. Not all horses will get along. It is unfair to force a living/turnout situation that is traumatic or unsafe for a horse.

If you introduce a horse into a paddock and see signs of significant chasing, biting, kicking, refusal to allow a horse to eat or drink, or overall antagonizing that is not quieting down within a reasonable amount of time, you need to intervene. All new herd introductions take time to adjust and there will be mild disturbances that may lead to minor physical marks on the horse. These are normal and will subside once the pecking order is established. If they do not subside or they turn more violent, a change must be made. If it is not addressed, you will have behavioral issues both on the part of the aggressor in the herd and the victim in the herd. The behavioral issues that occur in turnout can also trickle into the horse's human interaction as well. The aggressor may continue its aggressive tendencies in interactions with you. It may carry over its newfound emotions and power outside of the turnout environment. The victim or submissive horse may become defensive and aggressive towards you due to emotional and physical stress in the turnout environment. You would be amazed how a horse's turnout and living arrangements can affect their overall mental and physical health. Happy herd = happy horse.

Pulling while tied

A horse possesses such amazing strength that it should be no surprise that when a horse pulls back when tied, something's going to give. It can be a very scary scenario when a horse pulls back: the halter/rope may break sending the horse flying backwards, the object the horse is tied to may break and the horse will be dragging it behind them, the horse may slip and fall and end up hanging themselves, and on rare occasions when nothing else gives the horse may end up severely injuring or even breaking their neck.

Why do horses do this? There can be many reasons for this behavior: fear of the restraint because they sense they are trapped and unable to satisfy their flight instinct, lack of education and experience on how to stand tied, or simply a bad habit that has developed due to circumstances.

Fear

As discussed earlier, horses are flight animals. When anything upsets or stresses them they will try to leave. When the horse tries to leave and is unable to because they are tied, the horse may panic and fight against the restraint. Your horse's flight instinct is telling it to get away, but their head is tied so the horse feels trapped. Horses that feel trapped can be a very dangerous thing, they lose sight of their own well-being and will thrash until something gives or they are too exhausted to continue. With the horse that panics when tied because they feel trapped, it is important to develop a trusting relationship and teach them to yield to the pressure of being tied without panicking. If they do not yield to pressure but rather fight it, they will never tie well and this lack of education will rear its ugly head in many areas.

Teaching or reinforcing established training of how to properly yield to face pressure comes first. I also teach horses to stand still for extended periods of time without being tied while incorporating stimulus that may make them want to move. When they move I put them right back to where they started, this emphasizes to the horse that movement without being asked is unproductive.

After your horse yields to pressure well and is comfortable standing for longer periods of time with other stimulus around them, you can begin teaching them to tie. I begin by simply running a long lead rope (long enough that you can step away from the pulling horse and get out of harm's way and still maintain a hold of your rope) through a ring attached to solid wall and hold the other end while I groom and move around my horse. (Make sure you are wearing gloves when working with any horse that pulls.) I do this on a safe, soft surface such as arena dirt, nothing hard or slippery like concrete or grass. This minimizes the chance of the horse slipping and falling. Also, make sure you are in some sort of enclosed area in case your horse does pull away from you.

As you move around your horse, tighten and release the face pressure with your long lead. Find your horse's comfort zone. Start to introduce stimulus that may cause your horse to be unsettled, and reinforce the standing training that you instilled earlier. A soothing voice and reinforcing the command not to move by using a verbal cue, such as "stand," works well. When your horse pulls, which any habitual puller will do, allow a little give of rope through the ring until the horse quiets, then apply face pressure until they walk back forward, putting the horse in the same position they were in before they pulled back. Allowing the little bit of give to the rope will lessen the horse's panic, and putting them back where they were will instill that pulling back will get them nowhere. Using a firm steady voice and remaining calm when asking your horse to stop pulling is also helpful. You can use the word "whoa" or "stand," both are acceptable. Repeat this process until your horse stops backing as soon as it feels the face pressure and stays relaxed and quiet.

Behavioral

Your horse may also discover that pulling back allows them to break free and get away from situations they do not want to be in. Horses usually discover this trick by accident, initially pulling back from anxiety or a lack of understanding of how to stand tied. After discovering they can break the halter, lead, or crossties, the horse then has a go-to maneuver whenever they would like to leave. This may occur during grooming, saddling, farrier work, veterinary work, etc. These horses do not pull because they are scared or upset, but when they make the decision to not want to participate in the given activity. They simply are making a choice to leave. These horses are usually easier to work with, as we can discipline the behavior; we are not dealing with an emotional fear response. The behavioral puller remains in control of their problem solving and decision making abilities while pulling, so we can appeal to that part of the horse.

You can approach this behavior in several ways, but I find it helpful to go back and reinforce yielding to pressure, standing for periods of time while being worked with, and also going forward from stimulus from behind. I like to use a medium length whip, dressage whips work well. If the horse is not taught these things well in advance, you cannot discipline the behavior of not standing and asking the horse to step back forward. If your horse does not fully understand what the right thing is, you cannot discipline it for making a wrong choice. I tackle this behavior in the same environment as the emotional puller. A soft safe surface, enclosed area with enough room to maneuver around, and a ring attached to a solid wall to run your lead through.

I begin by doing an activity that the horse normally is okay standing for, then I incorporate an activity the horse usually pulls back to escape. Whether it's saddling, farrier work, clipping, etc., I stand to the side of the horse, as with an emotional puller, incorporate the stimulus, and then hold the line up front. However, this time I am ready to discipline the horse from behind with the dressage whip if they decide to ignore the cue to stand quietly.

Here's the scenario: A horse pulls back when I initiate the saddling process, so as I place the saddle pad on the horse's back I notice it start to elevate the head and "sit down" to pull. At this point I will start lightly tapping it on the hindquarters, increasing the stimulus from behind as the horse continues to pull. Again, a verbal such as "stand" in a firm voice helps also, if that cue has been taught. Once the horse quiets and stands, I immediately return to the activity that triggers the pulling, repeating the steps until the horse no longer pulls back. If the horse pulls during activities such as farrier/vet work, you will either need to enlist the cooperation of these professionals or simulate the work yourself. Using tools of the trade to simulate the activities yourself works also.

With either variety of pullers, this behavior is not easily curbed. It may take many sessions to eliminate the behavior completely, and you should always pay close attention to the horse's body language when tied, as they can fall back into the habit easily. This habit is dangerous for all involved, so be aware and make others aware of your horse's past pulling problems whenever they are in a situation where it may occur.

Cinchy horses

Your horse may exhibit negative behavior while you are tightening your girth for a variety of reasons. These behaviors may include ear pinning, tail swishing, teeth grinding, attempting to turn and bite, attempting to paw or cow kick, moving excessively while being tightened, holding their breath to the point of collapse, or just a negative attitude. The reasons can include body soreness, ulcers, poorly fitting saddle, uncomfortable girth, tightening the girth too quickly and forcefully, sores, dirt, or problems in the girth area, the horse anticipating unpleasantness during the exercise, and so on.

As with all other problems, we need to find the source. We address physical issues first. Check your horse over from nose to tail, paying close attention to back, withers, and girth area. Are there any injuries/wounds, soreness reaction to just your touch in any areas? Has your horse changed its eating habits recently that may indicate an ulcer? If not, we can proceed.

Next check your girth for any debris, hard spots, deformities, or any other abnormalities that may be causing discomfort. Check your saddle fit, if the saddle pinches or rests on the withers, this will be exaggerated as you tighten the girth/cinch. If you are not comfortable deciding on saddle fit, ask someone more experienced to assist you in your evaluation.

Next evaluate how you are tightening the saddle. Do you pull hard and fast? This can be unpleasant for more sensitive horses. It sometimes helps to tighten the saddle slowly with firm pressure, taking two or three pulls to tighten the girth completely. Also walking your horse several steps between tightening can improve your horse's acceptance of the tightening process.

Evaluate your recent workouts; have you started something different, harder, and possibly stressful, that your horse may be negatively anticipating? You may need to alter your workouts to include some easier exercises, something your horse enjoys and is good at, with your new, harder exercises.

After eliminating any other sources for the cinchy behavior, we can move on to disciplining the negative reactions to tightening the cinch. You will base your behavior modification on the reaction your horse is giving you. Look back at the behavior examples in the book and address them accordingly. Whether your horse is attempting to bite, kick, threaten with aggression, or refusing to stand still, you can incorporate our earlier methods, keeping in mind you cannot allow your horse to prevent the tightening of the cinch through the behavior. If you stop tightening to correct the behavior, the horse is being successful and will continue the behavior. If your horse is holding its breath, sometimes to the point of starting to collapse, and you have evaluated and modified your girth tightening methods without eliminating the behavior, we need to act further.

Begin by untying your horse and simply holding the lead rope in case your horse does start to go down, so that will not be a factor. With lead in hand, start to tighten the cinch paying close attention to your horse's body language and breathing. If you notice him starting to resist or hold his breath, you need to encourage breathing. Taking the palm of your hand, bump the horse in the belly, increasing the firmness until it takes a breath. Some horses may need a pretty firm hand to take a breath. You can also put your finger in the side of the horse's mouth and push down on the gums where the bit would lie (they have no teeth there) until it opens its mouth and breathes. If you are not familiar with this area of the mouth do not attempt it, ask someone more experienced for assistance. If your horse still refuses to take a breath, simply stepping them forward and back should help also.

You have to approach cinchiness with the thought that it is similar to you leaving for school or work. If you do not like the trip to work, have to wear uncomfortable clothes, dislike your job, and so on, you display a negative attitude. You are however not allowed by society to overreact or threaten those around you. Horses are no different, they are voicing their opinion on the situation. It is our job to make sure everything is as pleasant and comfortable as possible, and then go to behavior modification when they display unacceptable behavior.

AFTERWORD

"Nothing is more sacred than the bond between a horse and a rider. No other creature can ever become so emotionally close to a human as a horse. When a horse dies, the memory lives on, because an enormous part of his owner's heart, soul, and the very existence dies also."
~Stephanie M. Thorn

We have discussed many different behavioral problems that occur when we interject our wishes into the horse's life. The cause of these problems is therefore undeniably human error. We implement nothing but change into our horses' lives. We change where they live, how much exercise they get, what they eat, when they eat, and what they are expected to do on a daily basis. We put them in situations that go against every fiber of their natural instincts and habitats. It is our responsibility to make sure these changes are as positive and pleasant as possible. It is our responsibility to make sure we are improving the horse's quality of life, physical health and well-being, and ability to learn and grow in a positive manner.

Once we intruded into their lives, they became reliant on us and our abilities to make the right decisions regarding their health and well-being. If we treat them with the care and respect they deserve, the possibilities are endless. They will give 100 percent, all day every day. I have seen a horse love and respect someone so completely they would compromise themselves in an effort to please or protect their human partner. That level of loyalty is not easy to come by in our human interactions.

I can confidently say that this level of compassion, trust, respect, devotion, and willingness to please is why I am and have always been drawn to animals in general, especially the horse. There have been times in my life that I do not know how I would have gotten through without my bond with the horse. They teach us about true strength, love, compassion, power, and above all the ability to forgive. Forgiveness is not weakness, nor does it mean that the wrong has been forgotten. It simply means that the heart is willing to accept what has happened, learn from it, and move forward. I am constantly astounded at the horse's ability to forgive even the most horrific of circumstances. They are scarred by it, they remember it, you will see it in their eyes, but very rarely are they unable to move past it and forgive. If humanity could possess even a small percentage of the capacity for love and forgiveness that the horse does, we would all be far better off.

Now, sadly, comes the harsh reality that we as humans are flawed to the utmost. Humans have the ability to take even the most divine of creatures and crush them, body and soul. Not always out of pure maliciousness, but out of pure ignorance. I have seen and worked with cases that do not recover from the injustices that have been done to them. The emptiness in the eyes that so easily turns into blind panic and fear is haunting, for I know the circumstances that caused this noble and proud animal to give up and break had to have been, in simple words, truly unforgivable.

This brings to light again the reason for this book. I hope to never see another horse with fear, distrust, and pain in its eyes. I want every horse owner to understand why your horse may do things the way it does, what the cause and reasons may be, and how to rechannel the behavior into one we desire, without cruelty. If I have succeeded in helping just one person understand their horse's behavior and modify it successfully, without the need for fear and intimidation tactics, I will have been successful. If I can see one less horse with sadness in its eyes, and instead see the bright light of trust and acceptance, I will have been successful.

ABOUT THE AUTHOR

Nicole Brickner has worked with, trained and shown horses from an early age. Her mission is to make our presence in animals' lives a positive experience, through mutual respect, trust, consistency and compassion.

Nicole has been training horses and giving riding instruction professionally since 2001. She specializes in:

• Starting horses under saddle, without using harsh methods or harsh equipment

• Evaluating, diagnosing and correcting behavioral problems

• Finishing horses for the recreational rider or for the show pen

• Improving the overall relationship between horses and humans

She also trains for trail riding, showmanship, huntseat pleasure and equitation, western pleasure and horsemanship, trail class, hunter hack and much more....

Nicole believes in taking the time to do things the correct way the first time. She believes there is no such thing as a short cut or quick fix, and takes time to fully understand a horse and work with the animal to develop a trusting and mutually respectful relationship. In her experience, it is only after this has occurred that you can truly work with and train the horse.

Nicole tailors her training and lesson program to fit each horse/human partnership. She develops a relationship with both horse and rider and works with their individual personality types and demeanor to cultivate a lifelong partnership between horse and human. From the fearless teenager who wants to jump to the timid adult who always dreamt of owning a horse, Nicole has the flexibility and patience needed to facilitate lasting results and continuous progress.

Nicole earned a Bachelor's degree in Animal Science with an equine emphasis and a business option, focusing on overall knowledge of the horse, how to work with horses and people in a positive approach, and starting horses under saddle through finishing them for the show pen. She competed on her college western and huntseat team, and interned at Kasten Reining Horses.

Nicole has coached many horse/human combos to state championships, high point awards and year-end awards. She has also helped many to become as relaxed and quiet on the trail as they are in the show pen. Nicole has coached the Neenah Equestrian team for several years, qualifying for state every year and bringing home the division A reserve championship in 2014 and 2015.

Nicole offers horse training, riding lessons, seminars and workshops for horses and riders in the Fox Valley area of Wisconsin and beyond.

Nbhorsetraining.com
facebook.com/NBHorseTraining
nbhorsetraining@gmail.com
Twitter: @BricknerNicole

42079788R00081

Made in the USA
San Bernardino, CA
27 November 2016